The Awakening of Harley F. GoodWheeler

Harley F. GoodWheeler

FR33M4N Publishing – a division of
FR33M4N Enterprise`s Consulting Inc.

ISBN 978-1-67815-214-7

PREFACE (I)

Out on the fringe somewhere that is where I feel I belong. The challenge for me always being what fringe? All fringes? Do I wish to rebel for nothing other than the thrill of the rebellion; Opposing all with no want or hope of resolution? Perhaps I am antigovernment, and anti-religion. Both, so oppressive to my Freedom.

The epiphany hits me that this is what I truly am; a freedom fighter, a liberator of the oppressed, I wish to live free and impact no one. It is not a criminal anarchy I seek. Not some hell where only the cold and hard survive by victimization of the weak. The freedom I seek lives in the heart, the soul, the mind, of everyone and community is part of the freedom. Community where no collective oppresses singular existence. This is what I seek. The journey has already begun, and I will catch you up on the details later. I am on a journey to learn and to teach, to love and be loved, and to reach a point of honesty with myself and the universe, that I taste that freedom I search eternally towards...

A new person emerges from the ashes that was I... An alter ego rises to protect the soul. Now come with me and I shall share with you, The Awakening of Harley F. GoodWheeler.

PREFACE (II)

Religion is to spirituality; what a chain link fence is to an automobile...

Totally unrelated. In order to understand things in this book you must first understand that spirituality is freedom, and religion is the broad set of rules to control that. If you are a religious person, you may find some of what you read to be contentious musings, this is ok, it is our right as humans to have differing opinions, and learning of them is what offers us growth in the form of knowledge.

Spirituality has never had a commandment, never issued a fatwah, never condemned nor judged anyone else... These are religious events. Somewhere along the line this has been forgotten. Buried deep into our subconscious behind the guilt of sin, the hypocrisy of judging others, the greed of materialism, and a myriad of other modern follies; is our soul, our spirit.

To be by everyone else's meter a sane productive healthy person this is how it must be... so we march like sheep to slaughter some their entire lives without ever once reaching into ourselves and awakening the most powerful freeing loving energy and that energy is the root of us. It is us...

If left alone, starved of thought, we sometimes let our soul go back to this rest and we become complacent to its importance.

I first remember awakening myself, turning my thoughts inwards and truly exploring who I was, at eighteen. Due to my age, lifestyle, and exposure this wasn't uncommon although the circumstances were. However, by 21 I had become "humanized", engulfed in the facade that what I did was more important than who I was. Shortly before I turned 40, I began to once again awaken, in a manner that was derived as a survival mode to my sanity during a time where I faced great change and pain. And this self-discovery this awakening of who I am came pouring into my vision, my dreams. My soul is fed, my freedom to exist as me in a very technical world, only grows.

As we feed our souls or allow others to inspire and feed us; a true sense of what living with balance, centered and one with the universe and elements, is and we experience incredible calm.

We yearn for what our soul has been starved of, the elements and nature, artful expression and creative thought, all in an effort to "find ourselves"; and who we are finding is indeed us. The most pristine, pure feeling of one.

When we have no more strength to carry on in a world of pain and hurt, we either succumb to it and become without hope... or we rise. We rise through the layers of brainwashed acceptance and conformity... To truly open our hearts and minds to all that this universe offers us.

It is, what I call the awakening... in the great depths of pain and darkness only one can truly save us and release us back into light, and that is our true self... Our soul.

Introduction

Hello. My name is Harley. Harley F. GoodWheeler. The F can stand for lots of things based on what I have heard people call me; in fact, it stands for Freeman. I suppose I need to tell you a bit about myself, before I tell you too much about my Adventures.

I come from very humble beginnings. A very poor broken home, where laughter deafened the sounds of the screams. I battled homelessness for several years, addiction, anger issues, heh a real young ball of dysfunction. I overcame. I fought the world as hard as it fought me and stumbled my way through adult education, raising kids, a 15-yr. marriage, and a rough divorce. I had become a leader in my Information Technology Profession securing senior positions at will and innovating solutions. Adversity. I overcame.

Somewhere in that hyperactive world I once commandeered, I read of all things spiritual... I have never been a religious man. I am, however, very spiritual and for years have accepted and blossomed my belief system. I am quite sure I could fill a book with musings I have about all the great religions; I won't of course there are books out there for that and you would have bought one if that's why you were reading my story (an act I am extremely thankful for by the way, thank you for your interest in my exciting tale).

So, allow me to condense my entire life's work of knitting together my beliefs in one succinct sentence. I aim to be a peaceful, respectful, soul who loves with patience and care, forgives true errors, who tries to extend the compassion I hope others will extend to me. That's truly it. A living practice of this... is how I choose to live. Have people seen me as weak for being kind? Yes. Have they seen me as simple for forgiving so quickly? Yes. My patience has been mistaken as stupidity or naivety many times, and I receive at least once a week all the signals to know someone sees my kindness as me being weak and gullible. To all of them I simply chuckle... and hope one day they bask in the light of happiness that shines on positive real people.

Where was I? Oh yes... Just beginning to reveal who Harley F. GoodWheeler is. I am a mixed spiritualist. It is within both the pagan rooted Celtic land-based belief system and the indigenous cultures of North America and their land-based beliefs and teachings where I belong

I am a father. The children are grown but I have two. I was divorced after 15yrs of marriage.

I spent some time in my youth rebelling to the best of my abilities... Thanks to a once forgiving pardon system in Canada I was able to put that behind me. I was taught with great force and physicality through my youth. I overcame.

This I believe to be all you need to know about Mr. Harley F GoodWheeler for now... Enough to get you reading and you will learn more as the story moves along. Maybe somethings you will learn that I haven't even learned of me yet... that would be cool.

After a very long marriage, I exploded into the world like a young dog who got off his leash and taking a couple years to settle in to the new me... I won't talk much of that debauchery and partying though I will say it was needed on my journey...

I will begin this story way back in the fall of 2015 briefly and then jump to the spring of 2016 and spring 2017. Three or four years after the divorce and the shock of that had long since faded. Up until then I was a road trip warrior, hitting the highways of Alberta Canada and Montana USA. I was content to smoke and explore and meditate in the desert, fish in the mountains, but around this time my path was vibrating in my ears and I began one of the best journeys an old I.T. guy could have ... this is the story. My story. Remember that freedom is not a political state but a mental location. And getting to there can be the most soul awakening event you could ever have.

On to our first chapter, again thank you for reading my story.

CHAPTER ONE

October 1, 2015

I did it. I am doing it! I had to restrain myself from calling her right away; I want to make sure I sound confident and calm, even though I am a nervous wreck of the crazy adventure I have decided I need to live out. However, the reigning victory, has been moved forward as I read the confirmation email, letting Mr. Harley F. GoodWheeler know he would be flying to Raleigh-Durham, North Carolina for an October 23rd arrival. How I fretted with concerns that most would have. But I have resolve. I have resolved myself to finally following my heart, instead of logic or safe choices or protecting my ego with avoidance and distance. Not this time, after months of talking and pictures and emails and videos, I would meet her for real.

The woman who claimed to hold my destiny and reassured me always her soul laid with mine. Such nervousness, the type only a few shots of old Tennessee mills moonshine could calm...

After years of being on the bottom end of an abusive existence, this was my chance to do something for me, no permissions, no justification, just take off and see someone on the other side of the continent, and one country south. This would surely be the happiest time of my adult life; visiting the person who fell in love with me.

October 23, 2015

14 hours on planes and on airports and going through customs, 14 hours!!! Insanity.

After eating my LaGuardia airport roast beef sandwich and coffee (which cost 18.00 dollars US by the way) I was left with an overwhelming desire to get to the hotel. Oh, for the love of the universe how I have been waiting and hoping for this day. Travelling this far, for nothing but a visit, and the hope of something real in my life.

Seems I booked my room in a hotel in Raleigh in ignorance, not knowing that primarily blacks stayed at this hotel and primarily white stayed at the same name hotel in Durham. Bit of a lesson in American racism and hate; what a festering chasm of simple-minded rage and hate purveyed their thoughts here. No answer when I called her.... what the hell...

After grabbing a shower, and a nap I am getting hungry. I decided I will text her again and see what the deal is. I get her message back, thinking to myself this Love will be realized, and she must have just been busy. She asks for me to call in a couple hrs., "Fuck sakes man... I am here for only two days what's with the damn time wasting"... The inner, not fully tamed, me screams at myself. However, my reply was more of an "ok time is kind of short so try to hurry please". 1500 bucks on airfare 500 bucks on passport and hotel... Yeah... take your fucking time Mia... Take your time.

I walked over to the chicken and waffle hut across the street and enjoyed for my first time, the sweet and savory combination that is chicken and waffles... My mouth still waters today as I think about those first few bites.

October 24, 2015

Today I met my Angel... After more than a year of talking online and dreaming of this day, it was here. I was here. There she stood in front of me

And I cried.

Beautiful woman... clearly high on meth... clearly married. Fuck!!!

I tried not to be hostile. As we talked and hugged, I could see she wanted this life. But it was just a game not reality to her. Good she finally came, as we kissed a bit and talked, I felt all sexual desire and want bleed out of me... She was just another broken down angel, too messed up to have meant anything...

She tried at one point to put me in her mouth, I told her the visit wasn't about that.

I spent the last day touring North Carolina, headed to the Raleigh-Durham Airport

It was time for me to go home. The getting there was almost more important than the meeting my Mia.

I proved to myself I could follow my heart, go 'round the world if needed to find my sweet destiny... but alas, this was a wasted embarrassing soul crushing trip. And I feel so foolish. She was married and I was nothing but a distraction on her phone...

Perhaps I knew all along... after all for years I've had this raging desire to just be me, alone, unfettered, not shackled by the rules of a relationship. Yet I yearned for something, I guess I just didn't know what...

Upon my return home, I felt victorious, complete, and almost somber. It didn't matter who she was, what she did, this trip was about me, finding out if I could beat the anxiety, the agoraphobia, if I could truly pick up and hit the road for me... and I could.

Every woman I had come to know till now had been damaged, why did I always make such bad choices... Alas because I too am damaged. I wear the scars of a man who must be carrying baggage, yet my soul screams in my dreams of being a wolf, of running through the beaten snow... wild, alive, free. Free... in my own mind I realized I was never ready to offer the things I promised anyways... my journey has no feel of settling, it is just starting.

Wherever it is I will find this peace and inner happiness I seek, I will find it. It isn't here, in this life of mine. This trip was the first step out of this suffocating box I call life.

It isn't the love of one I seek.

Perhaps it is the love of myself I chase down... maybe I need to find compassion for myself, and acceptance of myself before I can try to be with another.

I longed to wake up with the wolves... fuck this flying anywhere shit... I will find what I need on the land, in places where my soul has always screamed, I should be.

I immediately have stopped drinking, feeling fooled was a part of intoxication... and so, my heart won't fall victim to my mind's insecurities any longer. I also realize now the premise of an online relationship is in and of itself outlandish. If you can not touch a person, communicate with your body and eyes and hands, they do not know you. How can you, outside of the obvious trust concerns in hindsight, believe you are somehow bonded with this person. No more of that nonsense for me, needs to be a meet you in real life kind of thing. This was a sign of growth I believe to understand that fear of intimacy from a horribly long, horribly abusive marriage helped me believe this was somehow a healthy thing was a self-protective delusion.

Touch me...
Reach inside my soul and move me
Look into my eyes and let me see the red-hot embers of your desire
Touch me...
Show me who you are, the you the world never sees
Let me give you my everything and seek nothing but your love in return
Touch me...
Make me want you, make me feel pain in your absence and excitement in your arms
unlock my spirit and fly with me in a gust of passion and want
Touch me...
Never ever stop....
...And I will offer up my heart and touch you forever.

Oct 31, 2015

Tonight, I burned cedar for hours, flames raging, and they came. I didn't know I was expecting them until they shot from the flames of my fire... Sprites dancing, the insane the wanderers stuck between, they came first.

The longer I stared into the flames the more they spoke to my mind. Like whispers in the crackling sound of burning wood. The old ones came, the energy of the elders flooded my senses.

I was being called upon, there was no more time left to waste on whores, and false dreams.

I needed to help others, but what help could a messed up half breed like me offer to anyone, I had been abused most of my life in one way or another, so what could I do?

I will always remember the words I held in my sleep that night, they have haunted me now since it happened, "you are the oldest of old souls"

Nov 1, 2015

I woke up and went to Walmart, bought 400 dollars' worth of gloves. I drove to the Boyle Macaulay neighborhood, a place I had frequented in my youth, the poor side of town. I offered gloves to everyone I saw with none... I cried how fast they went. I looked into the eyes of a boy who was scared to even accept them. I knew that fear. I couldn't stop crying.

Over the next few months, I took to trying to buy my fulfillment, helping with secret donations, I put three hundred dollars in a young woman's stroller at Walmart, as she decided which low-cost milk to buy. These acts made me feel happy but not fulfilled. I was simply sharing wealth I had acquired. But it was a start. Along with this I began smudging twice a day, after supper and again before I slept. It took care of the negative energy, but in my dreams, I was still a wolf... in a place I'd never been, with a pack and I was clearly the alpha. Some days I thought more about the feeling of my dream, then I did of the reality I was in.

Nov 21, 2015

Another birthday here. I don't know what it matters I have been feeling like youth is revisiting me. Like I am becoming younger with each passing day this month. Maybe it is some placebo feeling to help me cope, but I don't think so. I have begun evaluating my career as an I.T. professional. I realize I am offended on a minor scale when people ask me what I do for a living, as if the answer will be some measure of what kind of human I am. I have always loved knowing I make significantly more than most of the people who judge me to be less than them because of my humble appearance and attire.

These material things... these judgements for one's ego... this whole façade to keep us all corporately enslaved. Ego. It is a defense mechanism, yet in this world we see it as confidence... Ego is not confidence

Seeking to elevate oneself through the direct comparing or competing of others. This is a defense mechanism... confidence is not needing to observe others when one reflects on their abilities. I find little joy these days in speaking with those who lack the self-awareness to see the piety they show in believing they are ranked. The statement "I believe I am more intelligent than most" is never well hidden. its judgements and arrogance try to prove it, but alas, intelligence and most qualities used to elevate one's self worth, will prove sharing one's gifts, is the sign of having them, while showing and proving one's self to have gifts, is merely showing off to those who have not the gift, and acting shamefully to those whose gift is more.   Any form of belligerence, sarcasm, condescension or mean spiritedness is indeed proof that one lacks self-awareness and is still living to defend the egos vision of themselves.

I have been feeling change lately... can't explain it... It's like instead of feeling the wind or hearing the wind I am becoming the wind. No. It's like physical time and reality have become the wind, blowing through me. Everything is happening and life is moving as normal, but I feel like I am standing still, and the events are being blown through me. Like I may not even be attached to my body sometimes. I am feeling at times the way I felt when I overdosed at 18 yrs. of age. Like the visions and events, that I have learned were just drug induced hallucinations, like that is how my reality is feeling instead. Surreal, detached, I see emotions, but I don't know if I feel them... I have no reactions, just quiet observance and an overwhelming internal feeling that everyone I Interact with is screaming through their eyes at me for love, as if starved. It's like the world is filled with these once robust beautiful souls inside these wonderfully fragile shells, now scared, starving souls, falling into comatose sleep from hopelessness...

Too weird. Things have just been weird lately. This journey is just starting, but I don't know when and I don't know why, and I don't even know if it is anything more than my own slow fall into madness.

Is there a madness that makes you feel love for everything broken...? Maybe it's all from that damn overdose...

Don't Go

Come and stand atop of the valley of your life,
Look down upon its chapters.
Can you envision the little child?
Of such innocence pure, you were,
Before wisdom showed you as bitter?
Does your moment of musing afford you the joy,
Of reliving your heart first broken?
Is it joyous for you, your year's celebration,
Scenes of loving and laughing and warmth?
Enduring the punches of some lessons learned,
Can you still even feel the goodness?
Your story is hard for others to view,
Harder still to even speak.
For yours wasn't one of god loving lore,
T'was a life that progressively sickened.
The blood and the screams,
Of the villains you've slain,
And to innocence we shan't even say.
The valley of life is dark as night,
For you death will shine brightly;
Those memories buried, so deep they aren't real,
But they're good and loving and true.
You stand atop the valley of your life,
And you cast spit down upon it,
Worthless, shameless, is what you see
Think you deserve nothing more not you.

With crying eyes I see your life,
I look down and into your black.
There's no it gets better I can't even lie,
It'll get worse, this will be true.
Yet I want you to stay, come endure more pain,
If not for you, have it in my name..
The top of the valley you stand on,
The cliff's edge jagged and sharp;
Icarus backwards your goal today,
Diving like an eagle into flames.
I tried so hard to free you,
Convince you , tell you it's alright;
Still you look atop the valley of your death;
And you dive, take your final flight.
No more pain, no more hurting,
No more lies, no more blood...
No more loving, no more kissing
No more sharing, no more life.......

CHAPTER TWO
The Overdose- 1986

Cracks of sunlight sent brilliant orange beams of light into the room, through the seams of the thick privacy curtains.

Time was as salient as the liquid dripping through the hoses and into my arm. Struggling to sit up I realize I am bound, constrained and trapped in this bed I've just awoken in. What is this about... looking at the sterile shelves and unfeeling cold walls; I realize it is a hospital I am in. Raking my brain for some thin shred of memory some strand of recollection as to how I ended up here, I am flooded with shame.

I hear screaming and sobs, such horror when I realize the sounds, I hear are from me...

As quick as these images invade my calm they are replaced by more, and I come to realize how I got here. An overdose, a suicide attempt, my captors/caregivers have assumed. Heroin, Cocaine, Benzodiazepine, LSD, not even considering the hashish and the alcohol...

I wonder about my clothes, my personal belongings, does my family know? Surely, they would come to be at my side after this ordeal. But there is no one. A cold darkened room, machines beeping songs into my ears as I fade back out they turn to drums, the drums of my people, I can hear the elders singing, and I can see through liquid vapor trails my peoples traditional grave post...is it mine? Capped by a carved image of a wolf... my spirit animal, my totem laying legs up, and all the creatures down my grave post shifted to the same upside-down position.

Death. Have I died? Surely this bed and institution are not part of my path to leaving this world and moving on...

A quick tug awakens me and I see a nurse tending to my arms.

"You are awake that's good" this angelic woman with long dark hair quietly states, "you had us quite worried, people care about you, you do know this don't you?"

How surreal to have a stranger reach out with such compassion and warmth... Her job of course.

"Can I get untied please?" I try to ask with mild humor to show I am not a threat. "I am so sorry we can't do that yet till a doctor comes and talks with you... We don't want you tearing out your IV and injuring your veins" my guardian answered with a matching disarming tone.

"I don't want to hurt myself. Is that why I am here like this you believe I tried to kill myself?"

In this instant every nightmare that permeated my mind moments earlier struck to the core of my being. As every piece of reality froze for an instant as I heard the words "well actually sir you DID successfully kill yourself... Your heart stopped for 6 minutes after they brought you in and you tried to run away, we got you back though".

Oh, my fucking god... "Ma'am I may have taken way too many drugs, but I never meant to hurt myself or commit suicide I just took obviously too much... I died? For real I fucking died?"

"Do you know we found such a large amount of so many drugs in you, and your out breaks, well I'm sure the doctor will be by shortly but yes Chris... Modern medicine has given you a second chance and if you didn't mean to lose your life, perhaps this is why"

"The only gift I get and it's the gift of a longer sufferance... Thanks"

"Oh Chris... those kinds of statements will not have you out of here any sooner"

"Thank you. For your kindness and updating me as to why I am here ma'am" I understood she wouldn't unbind me... So, I tried in a thinly veiled way to show my cooperation.

So many thoughts so many broken memories I asked as she was at the doorway of my room to leave "how long have I been here?"

"5 days" she said... what the hell...

All I ever really wanted in this world was love... to be loved. Not exploited, not abused, not victimized under the name of love, but truly loved...held. Cared for. Such a tireless want and here I was... Recovering, alone, nary a soul to care about me. How had I lived for 18yrs and never received or been blind to receiving just a little warmth...?

I could feel the tears rolling down my face and I could hear my ridiculous sobs... in this moment I had come to the conclusion we are truly alone in this world... a predatory place where perversion and power and unrelenting cruelty was mine to defend against..

In these thoughts I slowly started to fade back away... To a wall of green... Cold mossy stones and chants, a thick fog, men is robes that looked like beef hide...

I was standing on the tip of this emerald green cliff looking out into a vast horizon less ocean... I could feel the men were having a ceremony...a ceremony for me.

Hearing harps play and a lone man, the Anam Chara standing at my side, "I am he who will guide you to your next world" this bearded stone-faced man stated... and all I could hear was the rattle... And the high priest again began to speak ""Go easy to the land of the ancestors. Let the waters carry you across to the Blessed Isles where your family and loved ones await"

He was sending me into death. Guiding me and as I felt the incredible urge to step off this high jagged cliff, I was stirred again from my rest... The doctor has arrived.

"Well young fella; good to see you alert and awake, hopefully we won't have any permanent damage from this very poor choice you've made" , ahhh he is an asshole...wonderful. "Ct scan will be back later today or tomorrow. I've heard from your nurse you believe you weren't trying to commit suicide. Is that correct?" I understood this man's approach direct and to the point...

"I was partying I ate some of my roommate's benzo pills for his schizophrenia. I thought they didn't work so I ate the bottle and then I saw the sticker "medicine takes 24 hours to take affect" ... And well... I guess I decided I better be ready and continued partying... Man I'm 18 and my life rocks I don't have a reason to want to die..."

What I didn't say to the doctor was what all the memories were. The waiting... the darkness the people... or whatever. Too much to go over it all again; but I would surely need to sort the madness I had seen.

I looked at the doctor; closely looked, a haggardly older man of possibly East Indian decent. What Bull had he heard from the years of seeing stupid young shits like me weave these incredible yarns of stories to get the hell out of here? "The nurse said I've been here 5 day's already. I am still feeling a bit tired and groggy but when will I be able to leave?" I felt straight forward was again the way to go. "5 days Christopher (to date only my mother reserved the use of my full name), you are indeed groggy my young friend, you have been here 7 days now and your interaction with the nurse was 2 days ago. I would say don't call a taxi quite yet. I understood. I wasn't leaving anytime soon, but what drew me away was that word Taxi... The memories. I was at some point in a taxi, going to or coming from are not clear but I am at a stop with the driver, asking me for money for the fare. I am holding a camera, offering a camera to pay and I have no money... why would I have gotten in a taxi with no money to begin with. Blurry, just blurry pictures with these incredibly intense emotions attached to them... What the hell happened to me... how long was I out there before I ended up here, I asked myself. Horrified by the flash of pictures that began to race in my mind, from laughter to heartbreak to anger all in seconds all with an intensity so overwhelming, laughter like madness, heartbreak like losing a family member, anger as a feeling of wanting to kill... These were memories. These were memories of my own demise.

I threw someone through a storefront sized glass pane at the arcade I frequented... my friend. I can recall his smile turning to shock as he realized I was going to push him through. I was in another hospital with my friend whose pills I ate, Ron. He and the nurse are making plans for my stay...whoa!! The mental ward. I was in a van...I spoke to my mother in the van en- route to the hospital from a detox center?? Why was she in the van? Why was she laughing at me? I ran I saw the run... Hearing phones that were the "bings" of an elevator I was on... People laughing, I peed...I peed on her books at the detox center; they brought me to her office I thought it was outdoors, but it was only a plant I peed in it. I exposed myself to her, accusing her of stealing every notebook I had ever written in, throwing the stuff of her desk. Such shame I can't express.

The running from the security through the hospital, screaming at the laundry cart person for stealing all my socks, and then that corner,

That hallway... Atrium type place. All glass like the emergency room but long in the shape of a garage, I thought ambulances must come in here, but I never saw the back wall or door, just glass complete enclosure by a dome of glass with white metal framing. Everyone sitting on the ground against the walls on each side, I sat beside a guy. I asked why the people were all sitting, and he ignored me, I asked what they were doing, and he quietly answered, "We are waiting". I told him I would wait too and sat beside him.

That disfigured sinister being coming over as if time stood still, like he was a reflection showing up in broken blurred pieces coming closer until he was inches from my face screaming at me, I could feel his spit, telling me I wasn't coming "fuck off you little half breed no one wants you, fuck off!!!" and forcing me to leave. He scared me to the core but I wanted his acceptance. The fading...blackness. Now I lay in this bed, which I realized came with a security guard beside me, and who would accompany me anywhere I needed to go.

I was in the hospital for 3 weeks, it was not until the last couple days before I was released, that I was actually sober and unaffected by drugs. I began to realize if I couldn't die; I could do nothing and never die, I believed myself to be invincible by simple attrition.

I know. I know what happened, at least my understanding of what happened. These scrambled memories over the months that followed started to form the chain of events that unfolded in my psychonautic hunt to simply get high. The events that occurred when I was 18 stayed silently in my mind for many years. Speaking my first words of it when I was 25 and then only to say the vaguest statement that it happened. It was 30 years ago, and here I am, with a destiny I believe that has had me living earthly lives before.

For a good long time, I couldn't really say I liked who I was, my actions were almost always with disregard, and be it violence, or criminality, or fatal levels of drug use... I made the mistake of believing there was nowhere for me to go... Heaven wouldn't have me, and hell turned me away. In reality and in full vision hindsight, it was my beliefs of those, heaven and hell, that had crumbled, but at the time I believed I was cursed to spend forever on this earth... not good enough to die. It is in that last sentence that you must see the pain I was in... I was not good enough to die. Such a sad statement to what I believed my life to be.

It was not until I was 24 or so that I stopped believing this and stopped trying to self-destruct with increasing levels of violence and drug consumption.

Over the years I have had short periods I believe to be flashbacks from LSD, where I become very disconnected from my physical world, and I explore boggling concepts and ideas. Unfortunately, I also have had times of total dementia, lasting only for seconds, where I have no recollection of anything. My name, the year, address, people, nothing.

Fix Me

maestro set the tempo to a manic, phobic pace,
you'll have to run to keep up as the Jones' have come to play.
slide it in, pull the plunger, check for heartbeat, push it down
feel the burning and the sting while it courses through your
Chakra
then I stop --- here comes the train....
Slide it in, pull the plunger, check for heartbeat, push it down
unbending at the elbow while the rubber hits the floor
and I hear the whistles blowing while the paranoia grows
1000 beams of light come shining through my pupils
hitting the convex curvatures, revealing my disguise
Slide it in, pull the plunger check for heartbeat push it down
all the blood that's on my nightstand while I push the needle in.
The mountain for my left arm, white and crisp and pure
and the Dragon for my right arm, bringing me to a wall
slide it in pull the plunger check for heartbeat push it down
feel the sweat run off my forehead
and I stop--- here comes that roaring train.
Slide it in, pull the plunger, check for heartbeat push it down
its madness and I know it, but I just can't turn it round
Slide it in pull the plunger, check for heartbeat push it down
that train just keeps on roaring through the space inside my
head
global understanding as I stand atop the world
a superman in a tiny land just waiting to explode
running, screaming, pounding at the doors of my salvation
living in the dark place and I run to each occasion
Slide it in pull the plunger,
check for heartbeat, push it down
like magical elixir it frees me from the calm

CHAPTER THREE

Feb 29, 2016

I went on a date today and met a beautiful woman named Amelia. A Cree Girl. We hit it off pretty well, we have a lot of shared interests, and seem to connect well.

April 5, 2016

I learned today that some of the things told me to on y first date with Amelia were untrue and have been ongoing all this time. Man.... Gonna be hard to trust now …

June 20, 2016

Been talking a lot to Amelia about how I love carving, would one day love to just travel and teach carving and spirituality. She is so full of encouragement for that. We have gotten out quite a bit, every bit of time off is spent together going places and doing things, a bit tiring for me, I'm not used to it. She is from up north, Wabasca. Bigstone country, so she is as fond of the outdoors as I am and since both our belief systems are land based, we have great conversations. I don't hold any grudges about the initial early on stuff, I think sometimes I see the worst for any infraction, when I stop to listen and put myself in that position it is very different.

August 10, 2016

I am getting a bit excited when I talk to Amelia, we are planning to find a way to start to make a dream of mine come true, but it will take a while to get there. Flip side of the good/bad is that I feel like I am being pressured about engagement, but for the wrong reasons, like not for any deep loving thing, more like a just to see if she can get me to. Not real thrilled about that.

Dec 15, 2016.

Went to dinner tonight with some people and we got onto a discussion about domestic violence and how pervasive it is up on the rez. All of them really. I explained in my estimation, we had gotten values crossed due to the catholic churches involvement in the residential school system, its systemic abuse and continued torture applied while in the name of Christ as an act of love, left our people broken...

They wanted us to drop our identity and culture and they replaced it with infection and emotional illness.

One of Amelia's friends; a Director for BTC child and family services asked me if I missed teaching i.t. courses as I had stopped doing so about 5 yrs. prior. I said not really but I did wish I could teach things of more importance. She asked me if I would be willing to put together a workshop on Domestic Violence and author it to fit the RCMP (Royal Canadian mounted police) ALERT guidelines... I chuckled a bit and said sure. Then something happened, as we were all dividing the lunch bill, I blurted out "I wanna deliver it". My friend looked at me with an almost knowing smile and she replied "if you wanna come on up to my rez I will fill the room with the worst cases we have", "think you really want to do that?"

"Definitely"

Dec 21, 2016

Why the fuck did I agree to do the so close to solstice?? A question for myself, while I poured coffee and pulled the sheets off the bed... drenched from night sweats. The problem with developing this kind of workshop is that it reminds me of so many things in my past. I can't seem to stop the manic thoughts and ideas and picturing the audience. Wondering if all that racism I used to face on the rez for being a half breed was gonna rear its ugly head. I am certain it will. Could be the silliest thing I have ever tried to do, but I want to more than I have ever wanted anything... something to help me feel again.

I thought briefly about my marriage, thought about my mother, the endless parade of men... thought about whether the secrets held so deep would come to light inadvertently. Would I be able to handle that?

And I realized, this was to be a solstice gift to me, my chance to really help the way I wanted to, on the land.

Finally,the second wind has come.

January 4th, 2017

Got word today that January 22-23 would be the first run of the two-day workshop, Domestic Violence, Breaking the Cycle. I am ready. How unorthodox, I will separate the clients, girls to one room, men to the other. As I play a video or have one room do an exercise, I will go to the next. Men and Women's were very different, it wasn't a matter of parroting in each room. I needed safety plans and women shelter resources for the women, abuse counselling for men, and addictions counselling for all.   I am almost thinking of it as a presentation, a play, I needed to erase that from my mind, and I wanted things to be real not rehearsed. How ready I am for this crazy adventure, I told AMA (AAA/CAA) what I was doing, and they gave me the time off. I'm halfway out the door of the greedy corporate life anyways. I have enough money, not to live lavishly, but enough to get by.

January 22, 2017

It's happening, holy fuck I'm nervous as hell, these are some rough customers coming to hear me, Arlene told me all have had their children taken, and all had been ordered to sit the DV workshop. These people were in the middle of crisis and the people who took their damn kids is who I am representing. Fuck...

Arlene also told me there were 38 people 15 couples and 8 single women, whose spouses were still incarcerated.

I begged myself to make sure I was healing, helping not hurting these people any further.

I put on my poor boy hat, my leather vest, took a deep breath, and began the march passed everyone to the front of the room.

THE WORKSHOP

I spoke of pain, of family secrets buried deep within us, suffocating our souls. I talked of the tyranny of the past, how we all still carry these wounds through the generations. I opened my arms and allowed me to tell me of their brutal physical assaults they gave, and the horrifying sexual and physical abuse they faced as youth. I heard of horrible sexual abuse from the women, physical beatings from almost all the males in their life. I heard of the addictions and self-hatred and self-harm, cutting themselves, suicide attempts, enough to put one into a CPTSD panic.

I soaked in every filthy, toxic, diseased thought and emotion I could... I've thrown up three times, in two days, as if I need to purge all this black out of me. I let each and every person take from my well, and I loved, and I cared, and I cried, and for the first time in decades... I belonged.   These were my people, my blood, and they understood me; they were as real to me as I was to them, these 2 rooms of people, had accepted me as their family.

Hugs, laughter, tears... all promising change. All telling me I had made a difference to their way of thinking because I hadn't vilified them. Simply listened and encouraged and suggested change... I changed from this workshop...   fuck white world. How ashamed I felt to be half-blood of the oppressors... but here I wasn't Apitow... here I was Harley.

Harley F GoodWheeler a man from far away with an honest soul and a newly understood love of this universe.

I was in short, overwhelmed, and emotionally stripped bare. Driving the 3 hours home I would laugh, then cry, then laugh, reliving every moment. Every moment of this new ethos. I DID HELP, and I loved it.

Feb 3rd, 2017

Arlene asked me if I could do the workshop again but up a bit more north in Cadotte Lake, apparently word was spreading about me and the Woodlands Cree First Nation Wanted me to deliver this workshop. I was honored and excited immediately yes, yes, yes, please.

I have quit my job; they gave me my pension and banked overtime. Having had that motor vehicle accident last year (Oct. 2013) had finally paid me a settlement, enough to take a year off if I needed to re-find myself. I am convinced now this is the path I will follow. This is where my happiness lives.

I have learned BTC administers 5 nations, so I will be booked at each one in the future if I agree to. I am so honored and so thankful to be doing this.

That guy I hate that greedy professional guy that used to look back at me from the mirror each day is gone. The easy going always friendly Harley has become the rebuilt version of a broken me. Extra note... I'm looking younger. It's like I am reversing in years. Too good to be true I am sure but such a wonderful feeling I have had these last few weeks. I have been developing another workshop, Addictions and Abuse. I am making a plan to talk with Arlene about doing the same with this one. I don't want to rush things, but I know the desperation I felt at the last one, education and compassion were in dire need and I wanted to be first in line for helping.

It used to be when I thought of my past, I had anxiety, shame, lots of shame. Seemingly when developing these classes I am able to revisit my past and speak about how I felt, what it did to me, and... A direction on how to heal... this is healing me; I am learning from my own teachings... if that makes any sense. I guess it does to me.

March 10, 2017

Was up in Cadotte lake, wow that's a very dark nation, but a positive is that all the women disclosed... I feel like that shouldn't be a positive, this shit just shouldn't be happening, but after years of acceptance of a lesser fate, this truly was positive as it is the start of change. I am beginning to feel this dumb notion that I can help change them all... just please universe let me. I have gotten used to crying and used to throwing up, these are coping tools for me somehow. The people here welcomed me like a lost friend, like a welcomed dignitary. How can our people have lived through so much, and still be so genuinely graceful and humble? And smiling. So much pain behind these smiles looking into the eyes of these be friend was like pouring their soul into mine and I would stare back and push positive light back to them. What the fuck is going on with me, this is so fucking awesome, I'm a people guy now... People like me... I was scared to leave my house not 3 yrs. ago and now I am rushing into the wild, into remote northern bush country to teach people about healing...

Been feeling some weird things these days, remembering conversations and laughing, having thoughts that truly have 0 judgement. I think as each little story of my life I share I these workshops it causes the shame to leave me... like I finally get to spend this blackness inside me on good. Not totally sure, but I think I am becoming happy...

April 1 2017

How I have come to actually dislike the church. How disgusted I am by how we have let people with no elected representation oppress and abuse our people. Calling us savages. They are the savages, hell bent and blood thirsty to force their beliefs on others. How funny that such ridiculous fiction had to be scientifically disproven. How amazing to realize every pagan, indigenous, land-based belief system in all of history observes the truth. Whatever a person's belief I will not judge, but when it bleeds out around me or my workshops... I will vehemently aggress that toxic bilge away from my people. Arlene mentioned to me via email after the Lubicon Cree Nation workshop that she is catholic, and she feels no mention of residential schools should be mentioned. She can go fuck a tree. Her brainwashing doesn't entitle the truth to be subjugated that's the problem in our communities our own damn people still believing the stuff that was drilled into them, yet they can't speak our own language... whitewashed is the rez title for that.   I am not sure what this will mean for my workshops or how much longer I will be able to do them, I am sad that Arlene is that way. But there are many directors at BTC and many nations in treaty 8 territory. I will not be controlled corralled or coerced. She wanted this in her community, and she is celebrating this professionally as if it has been her brainchild and she developed the workshops... well I copyrighted the parts that are mine and I sold the workshops to BTC so I'm not worried, just funny how one goes from being a glory hound to believing they actually know something more than the person who afforded them their run in the sun. My love for doing this is based on helping others, maybe I will ask her how many supports what she has said to me. Specifically, she stated "I don't care about our culture I just want them to get their seating certificates and get on to the next ones".   What a douche, I will need to smudge always after speaking with her, lest I allow her negativity to fester in me.

I want to make sure I don't get pompous, that I remain open and not filled with my own ego. Act slowly, react to nothing, and be sincere.   Love Respect Compassion. Even to that douche...I mean... even to Arlene.

Bad Day
Woke up to black storm clouds moving in
Guess it'll be that kind of day again
Twenty-four more hours of pain
And maybe it'll be gone, or not
Just another day of heartbreak
My broken dreams lying on the floor
Cold chill runs up my spine
While I have my morning smoke
She is the queen of irony
She spends her work on me.
Frigid droppings of rain or ice
Starting to dampen my hair and face
Another depressing morning
Another hopeless day
Turn the key to my ignition
Battery must be dead
No sense calling a tow truck
It's just one of those horrible days
They say the weather just might turn
But really what's the point
Guess I'll put my runners on
And walk to where I'll go
Surely the world will get better
And then happiness will come
Maybe I will learn to love another
And we'll still be friends - how grand
It's another painful rainy day
I think they've almost won
Just another day of heartbreak
Your still gone...

CHAPTER FOUR

I get asked a lot why I facilitate healing circles, and educational workshops. I am going to tell you a story about the house where I spent a few years growing up. A tiny little house, my Aunt June and Uncle Jack had lived there, and when we came to Edmonton we lived in a house on 37st an 118ᵗʰ ave. soon after my Aunt and Uncle Moved to a House they Bought In Morinville Alberta and we then rented off the new person that bought the house. I had the entire old garage as no one drove and I was the only man in the house, for a bit anyways.

I remember the night before my mother married a man from across the alley. Him and his brother drunk, fighting, smashing out the bay window, then the man who was going to marry my mom, turned on her, they scuffled and he slammed the front screen door on her arm trying to get back in after she told him to leave...I was 11 or 12 years old. The only man of the house in my eyes, was my job to protect my mom, so I ran from the back door and around the front yard. It was on the front lawn I fought him, me 11 or 12, him 32 or 33. He wanted to hurt my mom, I started throwing punches, going into the sugar ray Leonard stance we all practiced back then, I remember being so scared my 'dancing' was more like 12 inch jumps off the ground, stick and move , punch and step back punch and step back , I could see I split his lip, made his nose bleed , I went from a scared little boy, to a man beating another, much older bigger man. My secret for years was just how good it felt to punch this drunken loser and protect my mom. My mother turned on me, yelling at me , a neighbor came outside, a fellow named Ken Eiffert (one of the best role models I've ever had by the way) , came and roped me in, raised my arm in the air, while the idiot tried to get up off the ground where I had dropped him. The next day they got married.... wedding pics of his bruised lip and swollen nose... and she married him.

That piece of garbage ended up wrapping his car around a pole one early morning where male prostitutes were known to work. Shortly thereafter, he admitted to my mother he was secretly "Bi", and the divorce began. For years she had tried to turn me into a gay person, look what happened. Manifest your own destiny fucking with Karma, mama bear. All that trauma, all those days of screaming and fighting and blood. This is one of many reasons, I try to help and teach now...

April 15, 2017

Spoke to Arlene today, I was a bit taken aback by her attitude, the whole workshop and community healing had come from her, but now she was seemingly taking a rather egotistic approach, I feel like she is glory hounding, that is getting all the praise she can for these workshops. I don't need any recognition so I am ok with that, I just want to be able to teach and heal the way I feel I should, I won't accept or even entertain changing any of my materials to be more Christian as that is flatly what is wrong in our First Nations. I had last month began trying to branch out from outside the BTC CFS umbrella teaching Life skills Back in the Cadotte Lake Area for BTC Education. I also did domestic Violence and Abuse and Addictions for their Head Start Program. This turn of events though, a training centre built around my workshops, this is the best news I could receive at this point, and I accepted and committed to getting it standing up and operating. The Breaking the Cycle Learning Center was Arlene's Idea. For her constant enterprise building for personal advancement, I had mixed feelings, as it was her pull within BTC that made this happen. I have also signed to provide them with all the following workshops:

Domestic Violence
Abuse and Addiction
Child Sexual Abuse
Life Skills
Conflict and anger management
Stress Management

And one called conflict resolution for relationships, which I knew was not a mandated crisis area in any of the 5 nations under BTC, but Arlene was with a Man and they were having issues, I realized she misappropriated council funding for her own gain... Interesting, maybe I still am swimming with sharks, we shall see.

May 14 2017

I have been travelling around within Peerless Trout, Cadotte Lake, and Atikameg and Loon river Delivering workshops. I really Love doing this. It has become my new fulltime career and I am soaking it in. Having the ability to travel around and see the countryside, to visit elders I am meeting and to talk with people has been tremendous. I have also done some assessments for addiction and started doing one on o e counselling with high risk men, and at-risk youth. Talking to them about all kinds of things but mostly trying to help them deal with the histories of their own abuse. Sometimes I wonder am I treating assailants like victims... and in the end, I am. I am treating them like victims because the spots on their soul I am trying to remove are when they were victimized, well before they assumed the role of abuser

I have sat locked in a room with guys that have been charged with manslaughter, murder, countless firearms and drug trafficking charges. I can tell you I have only met one bad to the core person, and it was mental illness that made him choose his actions in that fashion. Could be that I live in a pool of denial, but I wholeheartedly believe we are all good people we just sometimes make bad decisions. The secret to stemming recidivism to me, is convincing these people that they are good people. This is what happens when they believe they are what others claim. Uneducated, unclassed, feral humans. The stereotype of all indigenous people. When a pimp gets your daughter addicted to crack and she becomes a prostitute you blame the pimp. The government treated an entire race disgustingly like savages and fed them alcohol on every reserve... but we blame the Indian right?

European hypocrisy at its best. An entire culture built on "Blame the victim".

What your mother was ass-raped? Oh, she probably was dressed like a whore.

Heard your car got stolen... you Must not have put your club on.

That guys a violent drunk, his parents must be ashamed.

You get the idea I am sure. A million reasons why "Wrong" is always acceptable. Easier to fight the victim they have less fight left in them. And I should be factual and say this is not just a European cultural phenomenon, in china 70 percent of the calls to police result in the person making the call being arrested. But I know, must just be all those criminals ratting each other out …. right?

This notion that the fearful may gang up on the vulnerable and make victims of them. It's a fool's game created by people far more strategic. Anyways…

July 1, 2017

Starting to get a bit tired from the travel and beginning to miss home a bit, I have changed things a bit to be running 4 days a week, so that I have 3 days off. With the 3 and 5 hours drives each week to and from home, I felt that was fair compensate. I have been talking with so many community members in the nations through these workshops. I have met the most damaged families in the nations and bonded and made some change. One of the most touching things I feel is when young guys between 20-30 ask for my contact information and if they can contact me for advice when they need to. I am honored to be seen as a mentor, a person they can trust, which is hard for them to do anyways, trust a half breed white skinned man is stellar, and it makes me feel real.

Funny in all my time in the professional world of Information Security and Technology; not a day went by that I wasn't challenged on something, bad mouthed, gas lighted, and always needing to prove myself to people who couldn't be half of me. Now I am up here in the cold and frozen north, and I feel more love and more respect than I have ever been shown. I matter up here. What I Do Matters Up Here!

No one can take the memories I am making away from me. And for the first time in my life, I feel like I will be remembered, when I leave.

Training Centre is going well, I was offered a room in the building to sleep, to reduce my hotel bills, however I tried to stay last week, and at 11:30 pm Arlene came into the center and I am not sure, but she may have been coming on to me. Was very strange so I immediately the next morning booked a room at the hotel again. Hope it is just my ego tricking me, I don't need anything messing this gig up.

Going to be doing a home visit for some one on one counselling for a fellow that was in one of my anger management workshops, he requested via his case worker and they approved. Out in East Prairie Metis settlement but he is actually a member of Peerless Trout. I remember him well, I didn't think he bought into anything I was saying, as he was fairly disruptive early on and I had kind of shamed him verbally to settle down. Was a good guy though, has a daughter a few years younger than mine so I expect that is the common thread he will want to discuss.

A Day at Remo's House

I met with the Case work Brody and his supervisor Trina at Their office about 9 am. I sat there talking with staff about some issues and possible workshops, counsel visits etc. You could feel the Lateral Violence in the air, it permeates the nations workplaces as bad as the oil and gas rednecks were back in the 70's. We began to head out of Whitefish First nation, each of them in their own vehicles and me in mine following. I thought it was weird that they didn't share the ride, but that was my inexperience, they knew that either one of them could be called away at a moment's notice this being child and family services, so they always travelled in their own vehicles.

We pulled up to Remo's house. A rather large full house, by that I mean not the usual single wide trailer you see on the rez and settlements here. The front door opened and a rottweiler came bounding down the steps. The two workers stayed in their vehicles with windows down; I jumped out as the dog didn't look mean, and did what I usually would do with all the rez dogs, greet him like a long lost friend, and he nuzzled into me tail wagging. I heard Remo "why the fuck are you two assholes here" he was looking at the workers, and he was holding a small 22 caliber rifle. My fucking heart almost stopped I felt my self-go to a whiter shade of pale so to speak.

He put the rifle down on the porch railing "this was for a deer in the front yard" he smiled knowing what he had just done. Brody and he exchanged some words, something about text messages Brody sent to him were antagonistic and meant to try to trick him into being angry and then losing his daughter. Brody didn't deny it. I stepped in a bit and Looked at Remo "Dude deal with your bitching when we are done, I came a long way don't waste my day arguing with these guys". However, while saying this Brody and Trina were going back to their cars, Brody Said "well she isn't here but we just got a call where she is and we are going to pick her up and take custody" both them quickly jumping into their vehicles, Remo reached for his rifle, I about shit truly believing I was about to be shot.

No Fear. Calm. Pass the emotion to him. Push the emotions back into him hard, don't let his level of anguish reach you. I intentionally Laughed out loud and said, "that fucking thing isn't gonna take out a fucking car man, what were they talking about your daughter?", "he nodded, tearing up. Seems I was part of a bait maneuver to allow them to come calmly onto his property, but they were really there to apprehend his daughter from him. Fuck. Fuck Fuck. "Why are they trying to take her Remo?"

He answered in a broken voice "she told them I use medical marijuana and they think now I am unfit, she is 16 so she doesn't need all the attention they say she does", "she was angry and lashed out at me". How heartbreaking, unfortunately I could feel his honesty. "tell me something Remo…"

I grabbed the stock of the rifle and giggled it "you even got bullets in this?", he laughed saying "so mooniyau has all the answers eh… I must be bluffing eh…. Like I'm too scared to shoot anyone huh…" and he squeezed off a shot into the bushes. "you're fucking crazy man, why did I come here "I said shaking my head and laughing, "you are fucking crazy for coming" he said, "But I knew you would come to help me if I asked. You proved that to me. You're a good guy"

I spent the next 4 hours discussing ways to contest BTCCFS's desire to take his daughter, I also took him for a drive to a gas station and bought him some dog food and a pack of cigarettes. He made me coffee the entire day, never once even asking what I took, just mixing it for me and handing it over.

I hugged that man, the only time in my life I have hugged a man alone in a house with only them. It was surreal the bond I made with Remo, in the end I helped him regain property in his nation so his daughter and him could move there, because of the way BTC divided up their workload, if he never again had an issue they would have no reason to look for him (or her). His daughter had come home just prior to me leaving, a vibrant beautiful girl full of smiles. I asked her how she felt about things she said "those workers don't ever hear anything truthfully; they twist words and break up families because they're jealous of my family. I don't want to leave my dad he has raised me since my kokum died.

I made two lifelong friends today. I helped two people. I unfortunately, also realized there was lots still to do if even staff were being this way. I would need to find out more, but for now I headed back to the hotel, knowing my life had been placed into undue danger to accomplish a rather sinister deed. There was definitely some loving that was going to have to be rained down on the storm cloud of an office.

Chapter FIVE

August 20, 2017

I did a workshop up in Driftpile first nation on Anger Management, they signed for a lateral violence in the workplace workshop for all staff of the band office and health department. I also have a date booked to begin workshops to BTC CFS about Lateral Violence. I was up in Loon River doing a workshop on addictions, and met with the RCMP, Victims services, and a few elders I have been convincing to start an elder's council. We spoke about training on domestic violence, on how they had not had anyone to date talk about how it takes 90 minutes to drive into peerless trout, so calling 911 is not an option in most domestic violence situations. While I was in talking with them, I got out to my truck and received a text, in Cadotte lake a bootlegger dragged a fellow bootlegger out of his house beat him on the front roadway and set him on fire. His wife and children were in house and witnessed everything. Still so far to go. I hope I see positive change somewhere take hold, it feels so unbelievably challenging and I know it needs a lot more people singing love respect and compassion before the common ethos changes

August 28, 2017

I heard through the moccasin telegraph (grapevine for everyone non-indigenous) that Arlene is trying to secure money from the Confederacy of Treaty 8 Territories, treaty 8.org is what I call them. She is trying to set up a training facility called the Urban Outreach and she is trying to secure the money to move into full on "in the community" training to all 23 nations instead of the 5 I have been doing. This was truly amazing news. If in her enterprise building endeavors, I am able to reach that many more people that is fantastic, best news I have heard. Or so I would think anyways.

What this will do for me is that if I work there, I will not be coming out into the nations. Now wait a moment. This is not on the path of what I wanted to do at all. I started all of this by saying I was taking a year off to try it and receiving some fairly good assertions the work would be here. However, this would not only remove me from the nations within the BTC umbrella but also some nations I am just making friendships with.

If I wanted to see as many Nations in treaty 8 territory as possible , this has surely come full circle and will bite me now, as if there is an agency delivering these in house, I certainly will need to hustle to get work. This almost becomes to me, a situation of leave now get as much work as I can while I can, or stay and when I leave here the ride is over.

To think this fully through would mean I need to acknowledge that these will be non-culturally based teachings, which means I really just can't do them and feel any integrity. The likely occurrence would be that the place would be populated by the more religious people so that would be so uncomfortable for me (I remember seeing bibles on every desk at KTC in Atikameg).

When you start to believe that church membership, sobriety, whatever you choose, makes you somehow better than the rest of the world, you only create a further chasm for yourself to drop into when the curtains get pulled open to your realization that so many lies and so much pain cannot be pure in its intention.

End of the Dock
Come on down to the end of the dock
Let's dip our feet for a while,
We can watch the waves til midday
Then watch that sun go down.
Doesn't matter if we stay too long
We'll put the world on hold and rest,
Come on down to the end of the dock
Let's hold hands, and laugh, and smile.
'bin a long time since we sat here,
too long for the both us.
come on down to the end of the dock
Let's dip our feet for a while......

September 19, 2017

Haven't heard much about the Urban Outreach stuff, probably won't until late winter. I have been doing the 4 days a week workshops, and have also began doing some stone carving instruction, mostly because I am looking for a reason to enjoy a hobby and hotel rooms are not the place to carve stone.

I Love doing this for a living, I sometimes think back about who I am, who I was, and I realize how hypnotized to convention I was. A walking talking cliché of every brain washed sheep on the planet, believing my ego of being "technically gifted", ranked me higher in the world. How disgusting I feel to think I believed, truly believed, that my success in my work, made me a better human. My paycheque the measure of me. That's ok, I am., learning to forgive my bad decisions of the past. For when they were in front of me, I believed them to be correct, too look back and change my mind would somehow make where I am less desirable. The path I am on is what brought me to here, so no regrets, it all happened for a reason. I may not know the reason yet, but the universe has eternity to present it to me.

Sept 25, 2017

Renewed my license to grow cannabis today, another 8 weeks for them to process which seems ridiculous for an annual renewal. I have a prescription for Marijuana, have for a long time. Was a bit accident prone when I was younger and have broken a fair amount of bones and had some surgeries.

When I was young, I smoked marijuana often, daily in fact from the time I was about 13 'til I was about 31. I had smoked casually or more like, whenever I could get my hands on it, since I was 11. Interestingly, that is medically, what started my prescription for cannabis. One of the misnomers I don't like about cannabis being legalized recreationally is that it is not harmful. In truth daily use of cannabis while a body is developing, can affect your body's ability and in some case mute, its ability to create serotonin. This is known as our feel-good chemical. It affects more than smiling however, appetite loss, improper sleeping habits, among others. When it comes to recreational legalization, I believe it should be everyone's choice and is a better choice than alcohol for grown developed people.

In Canada legal age is 18 -19. A male can stops developing between 21-25 years old and a female stops developing between 18-21. Given the risk I mentioned this means cannabis use should be made legally available to all women over 21 and all men over 25. The cost to render this gender-based rule however would be immense so a mean age of 21 would for me seem acceptable as most of the actual hormonal and chemical developed has rounded out by then.

While I am happy, we are getting closer to legalization. I do hope in the next couple of years they set the age of consumption to be that beyond the actual legal age to vote before they make it legal these things need to be considered. Medically speaking, I believe for most things it is a more acceptable treatment than a pharmaceutical chemical, for others, I believe it reveals how truly sinister and greedy the world truly is that the threat of death is extorted, with the poor used as disposable examples of why the ransom must be paid.

At least once I need to write this rant down.

October 20, 2017

We are closing the learning centre for a few months over the winter. Roads and such make the trek kind of difficult for clients coming from their communities and for me travelling around. I look forward to using this as an opportunity to begin to connect more with some specific communities and get a few more workshops done. I rekindled a love of what I used to do as a boy, make branch flutes.

I am making a workshop about this, I am also working on more traditional healing strategies, I am talking with elders who are transferring knowledge to me in a way that I am so grateful for and honored to receive. Elders ask me for guidance at times, but these are not Elders who have received Elder training, these are community Elders. A lot of whom were part of residential schools, and as such have lost their cultural knowledge and received no teachings as children. These are the people whose wounds run so deep the trauma they have endured is mind boggling. Their strength is incredible, and they have not been shown how to begin to heal. It is the Elders, the Children, and the Mothers that I enjoy offering anything of useful help to. That is an investment into our most cherished people. To be a warrior is not just to fight, to be a warrior is to love and provide for your community, and to staunchly hold the values your spirit tells you are right. I want to be a warrior. The New Warrior. To take fight at the illness in our nations within, and to pass healing and love and values back to those who had them taken. Yeah… everyone wishes well, this I know. I hope I can strive to become, the man I hope to become.

Nov 3, 2017

It's nice to be home for more than 3 days. I had been missing the dogs, missing the kids as most of the time back I was sleeping or reading and developing. A lot feels different at home. Quieter than I remember, the overall peace I feel inside is incredible and I have been, among the house cleaning and chores, carving, making music, writing, enjoying my time. I have realized this dumb ass Apitow kosisan has accomplished a lot, and it is a good time to have taken a break. I was beginning to feel very emotionally drained, empty and tired. The recharge will help with the next round and I have booked a few larger workshops and a small healing circle. In Driftpile I have a One Day workshop to give to 100+ people and 2 community engagements each for 2 days, one in sucker creek, and one in lake sturgeon. Bit of a haul but that's what I have the truck for. Kind of a laid-back schedule for the month but I am going to savor the rest. I am happy to be delivering to larger audiences and to people who aren't bound by a court order to be there, a reality I sometimes choose to ignore because of the response months after from some of the attendees. I find myself thinking of one young woman, about 30 or so, in a not so great set of circumstances. I hope she was ok, and her children were ok. I had written a letter to the chief of her nation asking that he find a way to encourage the band office to pay her to do local workshops in the community. She was well spoken and very intelligent and when I delivered to her class, she came to me after, saying she felt she could "Do my Job". I had heard they offered to pay for her to go get trained as a certified facilitator. I hope she is doing well, I guess I will find out in a couple months since January I will be back up and at it.

Nov 4, 2017

Heard from Arlene today, Urban Outreach stuff was tabled 'til spring. Fine by me as the learning centre has been doing what we wanted anyways.

Dec 06, 2017

Just got back from Driftpile FN, man I love it up there, very cultural and very traditional, not a lot of religion has permeated here. The elders say it is because when the missionaries came, they were able to hide in the deep bush. As a result, their children grew up in culture and that is the adults and elders today. Each Nation has its own story, but all were affected in some manner. It was a nice Nation, granted it did have more exposure to the highway then most, but the back country was great for hiking around, fishing etc. Peerless Trout is a nation when I first went, I thought fishing would be great, this nation has a 65km gravel road leading into it with no intersects along the way, just a long winding gravel road which, should mean a great deal of wildlife should be seen and even fall frequent victim to the road. But nothing, not once travelling up and down that barren road have I seen any wildlife short of some regional birds, but you can see the well pumps within a few km off the side of the road, industry has killed every bit of wildlife, and trout lake is empty. This is all results of oil and gas. It is a fact treaty were signed giving guarantee to indigenous people that hunting and fishing lands would be theirs, yet even the nations are not arguing back to the government for environmental remediation. Anyways good trip I delivered to Elders and Staff. One of my many loves is when going into communities insist that the events be catered by local cooks. This means moose meat stew, bannock, good hearty eating.

Been having a lot of fun in my down time. Life's a lot more interesting when you have given your all into something and the break comes. How absurd I could be so successful in i.t. yet have only really half assed my way through it- always about the ego, but now life is about every minute, and getting something out of it for my soul. I wish I had someone to share this life with, not that being single is a bad thing, I just have a lot of love and a lot of joy and no one but kids to give it to.

Dec 22, 2017

The kids' mother, my Ex-wife, tried to commit suicide today. Going to have to tell them.. anyways not sure how yet but I am going to have to.

Dec 27, 2017

Well thankfully, the kids aren't mad at me about their mother trying to off herself. Interesting point on that as you never want to say a person is doing that for attention, worst possible statement for those that are seriously considering taking their own life. I don't think that's the case here. The doctors told me she couldn't have died overdosing on the antidepressants she took, just be out of it for a while. He told me the bigger concern is bringing her into a sober state to get off alcohol. They put alcohol patches on her skin so that her heart and organs wouldn't quit, she was being held so they could wean her off of alcohol. Interesting

Dec 31, 2017

It's going to be a great year this next year I can feel it. I am in such good spirits and feeling so young and alive. Been noticing the younger women starting to look at me more, not that it's important to me, just I think I am getting younger. I seriously think I am stacking years onto my life. I get tired and all that, but I just feel so dam alive I can't express it. This will be a good year. I will make sure of that!

CHAPTER 6

The two previous years have been the most exciting of my life. I had to think before typing that, have they really?   You have been shot, lived on the streets, been on serious drugs and had an addiction, travelled around the world for the Department of Defense on I.T. work… and these two years have been the most exciting??   Yes indeed.   What I never knew 'til the recent past is that I had adopted who I was personally as a mix of the attitude of my environment and the desire to be a big shot.

What a relief to live a life of simply being me, doing nice things, trying to make people happy on a deeper level, carving, writing, while I look despair and ravage in the eyes I find incredible peace in believing I am fighting a war very few are brave enough to fight. The war for freedom.

I control my emotions, I control my direction, I control everything about my world. I suppose I always had but I let influence and jealousy overlord over compassion.   I love to smile…   I look at old pictures and my eyes look dead … my smile looks like I am breaking wind, not enjoying the moment, but as I look back on the last couple years' worth of postcards, I see the joy in my eyes, and I love to touch people…   not in a weird way, I mean touch their shoulder their arm when I am talking with them, it disarms people and they open up after I touch. It is great. I am learning how to channel the flood of pain I feel when I encounter a tortured soul, an abused human, I am learning how to stay composed and not get lost in their stress with the emotion, quite some time ago things began feeling like they were flowing through me, this is what happens with the darkness and stress. I feel it but I let it keep flowing but I try to once be getting an open path, push love and understanding back to the person when they are empty.   Takes a bit, and it tires me out, but I don't feel like I am shouldering the worlds troubles anymore, just one loving human at a time.

On that note, I am feeling like I talk in my sleep to people who aren't there. I can't explain, sometimes in the morning I am tired and feel like I have to go back to sleep because it feels like I have been talking all night.   Silly and probably just a sign I need to get back to full time teaching and healing.

Luckily for me that will be soon as next week I go up Sturgeon Lake to do some speaking. I am such a small and tiny being in such a big universe, I am sure no one notices me trying to be this weird light giver, I am sure the success I feel is nothing when compared to the despair that needs addressing. But I am trying. I am trying. I may be insignificant, but I hope there are others travelling around feeding should and fighting darkness. I hope we are making progress. I hope in the next 12 months I can help even one person. Every day I wake up and think that. Try to help everyone and if it works for one you have one more to fight with you on your side.

Seems the little lady I had been thinking about has become a local facilitator. I am setting up a round of community engagements 23 communities in 60 days. I have asked her to speak at the one I am having in her nation. Haven't heard back yet but I am sure I will. The start of my army of education,

ha ha... I hope anyways, if she was empathic as I felt she was, she may be angered I got her interested in something like this, but from what I understand she is teaching traditional parenting, and staying away from the sensitive topic areas. Seems like everyone avoids the hard stuff. Everyone but me. Emotional masochist....

January 15, 2018

Back at it up in the learning Centre; like some kind of loved routine, I go through the workshops, I don't really bother much with too much of the PowerPoint and projector business anymore, I prefer the feel of talking, just talking with everyone, I am trying to always form circles they are more conducive to healing than the whole square table square chair rows and rows of monotony business. I try to go through the slides and make sure people know the material but what I am really interested in is starting them on the path of awakening their self-awareness. Over the last few months, I have sat some courses and earned my Master of Mindfulness credential. I have also learned hypnosis as I feel it is a helpful next step past meditation. It is a very natural transition when doing group meditation to bring them into a suggestive point of reception. No bark like a dog bulllshit , I let them know they will remember the entire session; which makes some of them initially doubt there was any hypnosis; that's alright I remember feeling the same way when I was being taught by example.

I am kind of in a state of Zen up here that is hard to explain. I see the mistakes and the faults and the ugly, but in amongst that is this tireless never dying strength to carry on among the members of these remote communities. They are like that bunny; they just keep going and going. This is where we need to instill mindfulness, try to stem the tide of intergenerational trauma that continues to punish each generation. I was raped, so I then rape, then my victim does the same. It goes on and on, always hidden and always subjugated by the notion "I love you, so I am doing this" when that notion stops the healing begins. Imagine yourself trying to convince someone who has been repeatedly beaten and emotionally and psychologically abused to forgive the assailant. But they must. This is not a forgiveness that says they ever need to interact with them. It is a forgiveness that allows them to understand how this happened and to move on, without holding all the anger and darkness inside of them. Because it is that darkness and toxic mass that then festers and turns them into the same thing. You can forgive someone, but it doesn't mean you ever open yourself up to them, nor does it mean, you ever need to look them in the face and say you forgive them. They don't ever need to know. This is forgiveness that opens the door to the proper forgiveness they haven't been able to give; to themselves. The shame and guilt and denial of these events leaves us horribly scarred but once we get the darkness out of our soul, we can forgive ourselves for believing we earned, encouraged, or solicited such abuse.

I am hearing Arlene is recharging her push for the Urban Outreach. She has been cutting spending here, now there are no local cooks and sandwiches are being ordered in. I don't know how long I will stay here doing these courses, as if they become too littered with European thoughts of costs, and running lean, they will have negated any positive outcomes by putting numbers and values on people's health. This is exactly what shouldn't happen. I won't pay it much heed for a little bit and see if there is more going on that I just don't know about.

I have gotten quite few events booked outside of the BTC umbrella, and while I do not want to subscribe to or be a part of lateral violence I will say I am hearing things about Arlene that I find troubling, and I may need worry about at some point.

I also learned that one of the guys I have been communicating with works at a gas station. A BTC CFS staff member came and filled up their personal vehicle and tried to put it on BTC's gas account. This fellow called BTC to report the vehicle didn't match the allowed license plates. The next Day CFS came into his house unwarranted and took his 3 children from his wife. Apprehended for no good cause, they said they received anonymous reports. Well anyone with 5 minutes of social work under their belt knows you can't do anything on an anonymous report. This was blatant bullying and lateral violence. I find it interesting the this is the only staff team up here in the 5 nations who still hasn't sat my lateral violence courses. Arlene always has a reason to not book a date or move the date into nowhere. Maybe she knows I speak about how weak leadership is the crux of gossip and backbiting. That if a director can't create a healthy team environment, they aren't a director and should not be doing the job.

February 2 2018

I talked with Arlene; the Urban Outreach will be a go. Not sure when yet but it will happen. However, what a strange turn of events have led to some other things. I spend a fair portion, maybe 3 afternoons a week doing one on one addictions counselling. I have I guess had some success in the people who share their lives with me. Arlene told me BTC wants to put up a 28-day treatment center up in whitefish first nation, and the board would like me to run it. Top to bottom. Methamphetamine and a new drug fentanyl have been pretty popular up here, but alcohol is always the biggest holder of souls. So, a lot of the work would be dealing with alcoholics and a disease I have come to truly despise. But it would be 30-36 beds. That's only 30 people a month, not a lot of help being dished out in that capacity, more of a quality after the crisis kind of role. I am so complimented by the offer and the thought of spending the next few years up in whitefish. I have to give this serious thought and I have asked her if she could wait a couple weeks for me to decide and she seemed gracious enough telling me the board meets again next month so take a month to think it over.

Went out fishing on the ice on the weekend, got some big pickerel, and had a great time. I am learning Cree or trying to learn Cree to properly respect the elders when I speak to them. Some of them do not speak Cree a fair portion really, so it also helps when they see some half breed white guy speaking it, to motivate them to learn their mother tongue. Also picked some frozen sweetgrass. I have a life I couldn't have asked to be more perfect. I know that sounds weird. I shouldn't want to hear so much and feel so much pain, but it unburdens the people I am talking to and listening to, and that makes me feel like it is a small sacrifice for a greater feeling of calm and serenity. I put my heart into this, I don't like to admit it, but I really do.

CHAPTER SEVEN
Random Road Trip Files

I travelled down to Drumheller often. An absolute beautiful part of the Southern Alberta Region in Canada. The Badlands. Beautiful rock formations and prickly pear cactus littering the open ground unfettered by tourists. This has always been a special place for me. A place to wander off, go driving into nowhere 'til the truck would go no further than get out and hike. Like a desert but not a red sand desert. I would find high hills where there were hoodoos, and small water carved crevasses and caves. There are parts where the coal mine has left beds of black coal, with these islands of little weeds and cacti, and exposed quartz and calcite, as well as what would look like iron ore of some kind but when broken veins of quartz ran through. This is, for me, a healing place. I feel there are not just crystals but rocks and stone that carry energy. This place is the northern most tip of the Great Plains. In the summer a breeze would blow in the night. The sky brighter than description with millions of stars, coyotes calling to loved ones. And the energy, it would fill me, I felt I could feel a million old souls whispering in the vast incredible valleys. Harsh and unrelenting in the winter, at least until the chinooks warmed it.

When I came here, it was hard to not feel guilty that I would leave with more than I came, paying honor with tobacco, smudged, and myself smudging to cleanse and ensure I carried no negative. This place would fill my well. It would re affirm the love I have for this journey, it would give me the energy I needed to keep going on this path, and when I would leave, sometimes I would drive for 3 hours to stay for only 2 or 3 and drive back. Sometimes I would be there for a couple days.

I would sit and meditate, center myself, and then open my own gates of suggestion and vulnerability. I would inhale this incredible positive energy into me, with each breath not only was I gaining my strength back I was easing the pain of my own scars, the old souls would feed me bliss is the best I can offer to what happens. In my souls' eyes, they were feeding me what I didn't have before I came. Inner Calm. Inner Strength. The patience to rise above judgement. These times I visit I am weak, tired, or in self-doubt and this beautiful spiritual oasis gives to me. If only pictures could show the powerful energy that lives here in the Great Valley (where dinosaurs came to enjoy paradise, until the floods of ice age).

On a recent visit, I had smoked a bit of a larger doobie, and was definitely there for a few hours before I would consider driving. I tell this to be fair for those reading who judge, maybe it was the weed, but I don't think so. I found an amazing hill on the side of Horse Thief Canyon, a vast valley used by, you guessed it, horse thieves, in the 1900's to hide out. I had a small fire going and was not just meditating but trying to project my vision, my presence, and visualize the areas around me. I experienced the sensation I would feel in a recurring dream, of being what felt like a wolf. I felt myself running, seeing what I wanted to see on the ground, but through the eye of a different shell. Such an amazing feeling, such freedom. It was what I realized as I faded back into this reality, that will never leave my memory, two coyotes within 20 ft me, but in no way interested in me, coyotes are scavengers, they should be bothering me or too fearful to be this close, but for at least 20 seconds they hung around me, before meandering into the night. This moved me in a way that I felt so overwhelmed, I didn't know what to think, I was very mentally wound up, and I end up sleeping in my truck when I made my way back to it, feeling too star struck and bewildered by this, to try to drive. I had already known my spirit animal was a wolf. These were supposed to be the eyes I can look out with, but it has only happened that one time, and I hope I find the time to always visit here, to always see if it is my day to experience it again.

When I am here I pick sage, prickly pear, plantain (not the banana type fruit, a healing plant found everywhere where weeds grow in this part of Canada), if a piece of stone moves me too, I bring it home, like a battery of energy to be placed in my outdoor "Zen" area of my backyard. It is a place I feel I can be who I am without the need to explain or talk to any other human, where I can be closer to the souls, I believe to be around us still. It is here, I believe I will die. At the age of 107 and I will lay down in this special place and return this body to the earth. I have known this since I was Eighteen, one of the visions or delusions pending on your belief, at the time of my overdose, was watching myself do this.

Everyone in life, should have that special place where their soul can dance and sing and cry and laugh, and be thankful, for the journey they have been granted to live; and this beautiful Drumheller Region, for me, is one of them. I wish one day to bring the love of my life here, whoever she is, and not just share the energy with her, but share her with the old souls, for I am sure she will feel it with me, when I know she is my soulmate, I will bring her to this place, and we will dance, a laughing, bouncing carefree dance. Until then, this trek remains my own; to take often, and cherish forever.

My Castle

Embers of fires that burn for you,
smolder and rage within the gilded gates,
of the place I keep my secrets.
never have they quenched,
these acrid flames of desire,
that incinerate and erode my thoughts of others,
leaving you, naked, undisguised, as my only.
Like the hot and burning sun,
will ebb its way over my castle walls each morn.
So too will the flames write your name in smoky fonts,
etching an image of you into my being.
I will always be near you,
as close as the night-sky that envelops the kisses.
you send riding onto the wind of your dreams.
When the time arrives in your kingdom.
when the queen must meet her king,
I will be near you, hoping I am yours
fear not my wretched clumsiness,
the awkwardness that is part of me.
Accept me to the beauty of your within
and I will be near you.... always
and that great morn the flames will sing
Tear the castle walls down
and you will let me in ...
my sweet......I will let you in

Chapter 8

May 01, 2018

Community Engagements are here! My Favorite! For the next several weeks I tour a bunch of nations. Each Nation hangs posters, prepares local food, and I spend two days delivering workshops for all comers. I get to meet a lot of people and talk with a slice of every corner of the Nation this way.

As it stands now, I go to:

Loon River FN (Red Earth, AB)
Whitefish FN (Atikameg, AB)
Lubicon FN (Little Buffalo, AB)
Woodlands FN (Cadotte Lake, AB)
Peerless Trout FN (Peerless lake, Trout Lake)
Sturgeon Lake FN (Sturgeon Lake, AB)
Horse Lake FN (Hythe, AB)
Driftpile FN (Driftpile, AB)
Sucker Creek FN (Kinuso, AB)

Two days at each beginning in the middle of this month, 8 weeks, I will do two a week, then after that I got invited to spend time at a Youth Cultural Camp by BTCCFS to Teach the Kids some soap stone carving. That will be up By Deadwood, AB a place called Haig Lake. After that I will be doing some treaty day's events for Woodlands and Lubicon. I have been trying to find a used trailer, as this will be great for the Cultural Camp. Very Excited to Hit the Road for a while again, I love this time of year up north. It will break down to a travel day, a two-day engagement, a travel day, a two-day engagement, then a travel day to home for 2 days. Exciting! I will need to make plans for the dogs, get Trailer, and Supplies. Busy week ahead for sure. The Community Engagement will be for Domestic Violence, "Breaking the Cycle". Arlene has told me that some communities are even against smudging and to stay away from cultural sections of the workshop. Not going to Happen. As always, I will stay true to myself and what I believe the audience wants, to aid them in their healing journey. You cannot "Ignore" the damage the churches have caused and believe you are breaking any cycle. Given that was the start of the problems, the coming of the missionaries and church, I wasn't about to bend on commentating on that. Our Prime Minister had issued an apology, The Truth and Reconciliation Commission was formed with 94 calls to action, but actual members within the community still try to pretend nothing happened and they are just god-fearing souls, evolved from savagery and happy and grateful. These are the same people who hide alcohol addiction. Keep their children's drug addictions secret, instead of finding help, s as not appear to be anything but a driven white snow pure Christian family.

Shit, I am going to need to go buy a few hundred pounds of stone, and carving tools as well. Definitely, the busy times are upon me. YAY!!!

Bad Guy

Cover me, be the second I need to be whole
Guard me from my own reckless ways
Love me the way no other has,
With acceptance, and a smile
Feel me; feel that I am but a low-brow tough guy
That my cruelty displayed
Is not as fatal as the cruelty I use to punish myself
Know I am the folly to my own biggest goals
That I push myself to the ground,
When I think I am rising too fast
Understand, and love me,
love me through the self-loathing I have
Carry me up to reality when I plummet
Show me you understand my depravity
Make love to me, be mine
Rip heart from soul and blow my mind
Make love to me, and simply mean it...
Cover me, be the one who sees me
Sees more than the mirror allows even I
Take the stains and the screams, and the pain
Hold them close, and show me they brought me to you
Wretched, Dangerous, Maligned
Don't use these words to describe me
Use Dark, Mysterious, even Romantic.
Just choose to be my love,
And judge me not...

May 12, 2018

I am leaving in a couple days, have most of my ducks in a row, and feel both prepared and well rested. This will be an interesting trip, will have to get the trailer renovated on my off time, as I kind of got stiffed on what I bought. Thought I bought a mid-80's trailer, turns out the frame is to a mid-seventies trailer and the shell is to a mid-eighties trailer, by the motor vehicles description that means a mid-seventy trailer. Either way I need to renovate it and do a bit of welding on the frame, and some roof restoration. I see it as being black with a red stripe, the death star... but for now it is sun faded trailer off white with a bleached pink almost faded stripe. Looks like it will be Loon River First, and I can't wait to get up there.

May 18, 2018

I delivered in Loon River. Interesting place, definitely primarily Christian based in the band office, I could see some cringe when I explained how intergenerational trauma came to be. But I saw no one, dispute the scars towards the end. I talked with the local psychologist, explained to her in vivid detail my thoughts on where the problem in our communities are, she expressed this was the first time she had sat a full-blown break down of events from a holistic level, she always felt. She said that everyone had been victimized within the nations, suspecting 100 percent saturation of sexual and physical abuse. In this community I would not dispute the numbers, for certain. She thanked me and asked for my contact information, and if I was ok that she may call with her more problem clients that needed more education and healing. Of course, I agreed and happily gave her my contact info. There was a little dog running around, I was surprised, but as it turns out it was a band office employees' pet. Smaller Dogs stood no real chance against the large breed feral rez dog packs. I mention this due to a fairly new friend I have just made.

It was very muddy in and out of Loon River, a short but very soft and muddy 7 km gravel road. I had slowed down on the side of the road as one of the big lab crosses' I was playing with when I arrived was off in the drainage ditch of the gravel road, really just a huge mud bog, he was facing a Pitbull shepherd cross and they stood about 6 feet apart. I thought I would break up the fight if I needed to, it would break my spirit watching them rip each other to pieces. I have a couple twin packs of cheeseburgers from the Loon River Truck Stop and opened them and started on foot down the mud slide of a shoulder on the other side of the road. As I got closer, I realized they were going to fight but not without reason, they both were taking jabs at a little dog, some kind of terrier, I think. The little guy would get nipped hard by one and try to swing around and get bit by the other. I had seen this once, before I could intervene, and the two large dogs had completed tore a small poodle type dog into two. I didn't want that happening here. I screamed at the dogs to get their attention waving the cheeseburgers, fearful I might get attacked. I had both their attention and I threw three cheeseburger patties as far away as I could but still down in the muddy drainage ditch. They tried to outrun each other slogging thru the mud to get their free lunch, I approached the little dog, and gave him the bottom bun and burger. As he took it I pulled him up and out of the mud, with the light drizzle falling I got most of the dirt off of him and into my truck. Well shit. What a cutie, very scared and quite obviously a pup who shouldn't be running with the big dogs of the rez. Almost immediately I knew my two dogs at home, having recently lost their lifelong sibling, would likely be a bit surprised by their new young roommate. Hell, yeah, he was coming home with me. I stopped in slave lake bought a bag of food and tried to coerce him to eat some real dog food, he finally began to do so, and I sang old classic rock tunes for the two hours into Slave Lake, he had seemed to be almost grateful, like he knew he had just been saved a rather horrible fate.

I decided halfway between Edmonton and Slave lake Sammi would be his name. He was such a timid little guy, I could see he was not even a little trusting of humans, but he was settling in to at least riding with me. So, a quick stop home to drop him off then back up to Cadotte Lake

May 19, 2018

Sammi seems very respectful towards his new family and has seemingly not quite understood this is his new home, no take backs. I wanted to take him back on the road with me to get to know him, but he gets scared stiff at the mention of going outside, even just to pee. I guess he figures he got in, and he isn't going out. Funny little guy, so he will stay with the other two and my daughter, while I head back.

Headed to Cadotte Lake, Woodlands Cree Nation. While I was in Loon River, a person had been beaten to death and another stabbed to death. Will be a somber somewhat uneasy first day I suspect. These are the kind of things I need to be prepared for when doing community engagements. Lubicon had already rebooked a day later because the community will be shut down for an elder's funeral. It is very customary for the entire community to shut down when an elder or respected community member passes. There is usually a 24 hour a day wake until the funeral, during which time family members, community, and friends will gather to pay their respect and help the family while they grieve. Something that also happens far too often in these communities, loss. I have had a lot of requests to talk of bereavement and loss, but I am not ready to yet, I have to think more on the delivery. I would like to instead design a healing circle for discussing the loss of loved ones, I will put that on the horizon and see if I can find a time soon to do that. The countryside up here and constant fresh air is absolute euphoria on the senses. Hope that Sammi fella does ok for a bit.

june 31, 2017

I spent the last week up in a place called Deadwood Alberta, having some soap stone carving sessions with some fosters kids at an annual BTC cultural camp

I also brought one of my dogs for the week Ginger. A little yorkie cross Girl I have had forever; she gets insulin twice a day as she is diabetic. She has also been going blind and this was her last trip.

A lot of fun was had over the week, did some boating around the lake, was given the honor of the rabbit head in my rabbit soup, the brains are a delicacy but I did raise some eyebrows as I also eat the eyes and tongue. Little ginger has been given half of a moose leg bone and has furiously been chewing away on it. I have talked to so many people here, including a counselling session for a family. The downside to being here is going back to Cadotte Lake to the BTC trailer to shower, what a Bat Haven that is. So, for now I jump in the lake to bathe.

Chapter 9 Rough Memories... Always in the morning

Violence is a hard path to choose voluntarily. At the start of a violent life, it is usually being the victim of violence, or watching a loved one succumb to it. If we don't take control of our emotional reigns, we are sure to also perpetrate it; and perpetuate it. During my teen years I remember feeling anger in groups like a shark swimming around the anger chummed waters, I would eat it in, from everyone I could. Like a shark when full I would explode in challenge of whatever small trigger, I deemed acceptable. I sometimes wake up with these times in my head. Such sorrow and shame I can hardly move; emotionally and almost physically paralyzed by the overwhelming guilt. In youth I could justify the violence for it was always only a reaction to someone else's aggression. In my adulthood, I have come to see it as passive aggressive behaviors during a time of drug induced mental impairment.

But the memories of being a boy... so clear in my mind. I remember being 6 or 7 , my Aunt Debbie, then I believe about 13 or 14, forcing me to watch her, she would stand on her head, her nightie falling down, she wore no under garments, she would laugh and tell me, "Come kiss it while I am standing on my head" was like a funny game I believed, I remember most times after she would fiddle with my pajamas and pull my genitals out, she would "Kiss them" back, telling me to put my fingers in her, while she did.

When her, my aunt kimmy, and my sister would watch me (they would give me orders and bully me about as a little boy, except for auntie Kimmy. I believe my aunt Debbie was in charge), this would always happen. She would make me suck on her nipples and call me "Baby" "Baby suck them", she was trying to be grown up or something. My Aunt Kim, I believe, Never knew any of this, though she was younger than her sister Debbie, she was always the one who truly cared for me, treated me like I was supposed to be treated, demanded manners, and that I clean my room, and when the other two would hurt me and I would cry, she would come and hug me and ask what happened. My sister was as much an abusive sibling as one could be. I remember she would turn off the light when I was in the bathtub, sometimes being in the bathroom and screaming to scare me after a few moments, and sometimes she would just leave me there, until I began to yell. Her and my aunt Debbie played a game once, while I was In the tub, they came in and told me my mom and dad died in a car crash and weren't coming home, then after I was crying they laughed at me and called me a baby, then said they were happy they were dead and laughed... finally they admitted it was a lie, but then teased me more saying no the lie is they are alive..

I remember believing this was a special game, this flashing and mutual touching from my aunt, I was proud to have a secret game with my aunt, it made me feel somehow wanted, such a young age however, I understood nothing of the sexual implications, and often I wonder if my aunt did. When we grew up, I visited her and her husband, I was 19, she was 26 or so. Her husband Danny was a cowardly fellow of about 31 or so. He was ok to talk and party with, but just a bit of an oddball. They asked, after an evening of smoking hash, and drinking if we could have a threesome, I declined , however once Danny passed out, Debbie grabbed me and pushed her tongue in my mouth, she grabbed at my crotch, I grabbed at hers, pulling her blouse off we had very rough very noisy sex on her couch, her hubby never waking. But this was for revenge. This was a twisted action, from both of us, to do this simply to upset my father, her stepbrother. He was owed a lot of abuse from a lot a people, but this was my first time acting out an emotional attack against him. It wouldn't be the last, and it was also going to be physical. Revenge. Eye for an eye.

This was my youth, so angry, and so wanting to stand toe to toe with every adult who ever hurt me, exploited me, or mistreated me. This man, this Irish ego maniacal narcissist I got to call dad for a short time, he was at the top of my list from age 15 until age 20 or 21, after which I pitied him more than I could ever hate him. Of all the forgiveness, I had to give, in order to forgive myself and move on in this journey, this was the hardest person for me to forgive. While his mistreatments were never to the total count of what my mother attempted with me, it was him, I had the most trouble with. Understanding forgiveness given, never needs to be given to the person verbally, simply your spirit forgiving them, but knowing it is healthier to never speak to or have contact with them again, is part of that forgiveness. When it comes to being born into violence, I care not what my father went through, but I was extremely angry for what he had put me through, and he would learn I was in every way more of a man then he could ever ask to be. As quickly as he left me for the wolves, I did come back, and I am the leader of my pack. He would get his. In my old way of living I would have hunted him down and beat him as badly as he damaged me; but my battle this time was cerebral, I wanted him to know I was quite simply a better human period. Stronger, sure, tougher, sure, but I wanted him to see he never deserved to be in my presence, that every obstacle he provided with joy for me, I had overcome, to become a better man, a better father, a better human. It was my desire that he somehow find out of my success in I.T. simply to show him I made more money than him. And I wanted him to see that I voluntarily walked away from his white world, to become successful in human terms. Truly I wanted and still want, for him to see I am capable of being the violent cold beast he is, but chose to rise above his evolutionary perch, to become a better man, to show that while he deserved the most brutal of beatings from me, what he would get is compassion and pity. Something he could never offer anybody himself.

Broken Beast

> *An uncivilized, un-socialized, wreck of a beast*
> *Broken, inconsolably...*
> *No one knows the beast's pain*
> *Afraid to look into his eyes*
> *Seeing a vulgar brute of a being*
> *No feelings he could have*
> *The beast never loved, never lost*
> *Incapable of feeling such things*
> *Broken, like a cold stone shatters when thrown*
> *You know only what you're taught in this life*
> *And the beast knows misery and pain*
> *If a single kind soul could look upon him*
> *And offer him the kindest hand*
> *He would hurt it, destroy it, wreck it*
> *He's broken.... Shattered, alone*

Chapter 10 – The Northwest

I have begun to do some work on a more regular basis up in the Sturgeon Lake Cree Nation Area. Having done a 3-day opioid conference, then the following month doing an interservice memorial service. I feel very connected here. I wandered down to the lakeshore, where the burial site for the nation resides. I smudged and prayed and began meditating. This time I could feel the winds blowing through me, in a way I know only to be spirits. I felt such immense acceptance here by myself, it was the strangest thing, I began to cry, it felt like 40 years' worth of pain was being released. I was being hugged. The spirits of this sturgeon lake community welcomed me, they told me I belonged here. They forgave me for the carrying the blood that was so hurtful to them. They told me I was part of this place. I also ventured again into horse lake, to do some workshops on Addiction. My finances are in ruins, I need to figure out how to fund the continuance of this journey or I need to end it.

The last thing I want is for money to be the reason I stop doing what I am loving. The time has come for me to accept the fact that I may need to do some other work on the side, while I try to build a business doing what I love. I will have to find a solution.

I am getting ready to wrap it up for the fall winter, take the safe gigs on the winter roads, but it slows down up here during the winter months.

I have been really focusing on how having hobbies and working with your hands and mind can help you through some of the struggles we deal with when we embrace healing. I have also been up to Kapawe'no and done some flute making classes. I am really enjoying teaching some craft type things while talking and trying to counsel people. This seems like such a natural way t promote self-care and healing. I will be coming out hard on this front, next season, and try to keep refocusing the effort I give to the areas where I feel the universe is in agreeance with me.

I am not really keeping an active log now, just keeping track of my travel by my invoicing and hotel bills. I could never ever tell a soul that one can just get to a point where they are "Healed", perfectly repaired.. we are always healing, from the second we face the trauma of being vaulted from our mother womb, we are healing. Instead I will say I have reached a point in my healing journey where I am giving back in a far more productive way, and I spend less and less time worrying about things that were bygone. I sleep better, I try very hard and don't seem to have many ego "blow outs" these days.

I found my utopia, in this often maligned, and more often mistreated community of treaty 8, I have found myself. So, this break I decide how to approach the next season, with as much passion and joy as I can muster, for its all about the living now.

Chapter 11 – The Boy No One Remembered

How I have lost so many memories, I do not know. Drugs, Trauma, I have flashes of mere minutes in a life that lasted years. I paint this story, of this uniformly tight, balanced I.T. Professional who just walked away from it all, so rare to think of the oath that led me to there. The Walk towards my Finite moments of greatness.

There was a man before him. More broken than whole. A Broken Soul who endured so much pain yet held an ever-present attitude and ethos of superiority. Back when I was young you got bullied or you were a bully, always both, that was life. As much as the monsters in this world marched into my twisted boyhood, I predated in my prime.

Whenever I fall back to thinking about these times, I first always remind myself of the pain I imposed, of the violence I fostered. It is the hardest part of recovery for me. To Know the amount of pain I endured as a victim, can never be pitied because of the pile of victims I created in my wake. For them I give my regret, my pity. But for people like the man I once was, the only pity deserved is for the boy I was before innocence was removed. That little guy had such a tough road.

Like bullets through a smoking barrel, the thoughts flood me in random succession, telling a story with no moral or plot.

Once in grade 5 my mother beat me outside of our apartment building for catching me kissing a girl with my shirt off (was summer).. emasculate… that was her thing. Wanting so badly to "Turn" me into a homosexual so as to get even with my father. An evil woman's pawn in an evil woman's world. A year later I was in Morinville, visiting my Auntie and Cousins. A neighbor girl came to the front door to come get me, I was upstairs, so I started down the stairs, and things went white for a second.

My mother, also upstairs, heard the door and was in the hallway behind, I hadn't noticed, but as I was went down a couple of stairs she proceeded to slap the back of my head which caused me to wipeout down the stairs and lose consciousness for a few moments. When things were coming clear I could see the girl, Tammy Barringer, crying in the doorway while my mother called me a little faggot, yelled at me to get up, yelled I was an ignorant prick like my father. I heard those statements a lot in my youth.

I remember her making me come out to the living room one night and made me sit with her and watch a movie. Cruising, with Al Pacino. A movie about gays. I remember her wearing this fuzzy blue terry cloth kind of jumper pajama thing on the couch beside the way she sat with one leg bent at the knee, the whole in the center of her crotch facing me , I could see her vagina, it was glaringly obvious in hindsight. With her legs open like that I remember looking at me during some scene of the movie that was gay men engaging in sex, she asked me "how do you like this movie?" "is your little dick getting hard watching that?" and grabbing my genitals though my pjs. I wasn't, I'm not even sure I was old enough to get one frankly, she put her hand down the front of her towards her crotch and the big hole, " maybe I should teach you how to eat my pussy then, so I can enjoy the movie. Bit blank here on memory of how the whole event ended, I know I was sent to my room and back to bed, but I don't recall much after that exchange. The place I visited when she pushed me down the stairs was my auntie June and uncle jacks house, where my cousin victor, and our other cousin's victor and joey, and my uncle David, all lived. My aunt used to make us go dumpster dive the towns IGA grocery store at different times through the week, we would get bananas, Eggs, Old Cheese, and various fresh type foods. We ate a lot of Banana Bread and a lot of pickled eggs.

I loved visiting here, to be near my family, and boys all my age, was something I cherished. The fist fights, and arguments, and dirt bike races, the girl chasing and the weed we tried to beg borrow or steal to get... The absolute lack of physical abuse. In my Uncle Jacks House, Aunt June ran the show, and when she quietly asked us to do anything, we did it without hesitation. She loved on all of us, she could smack you in the head if you did something stupid or gave her attitude, but she was my family's caring sweet angel, looking after all of us lost boys, the blackest sheep of the bloodline always ended up living with Aunt June and Uncle Jack for a while.

I stopped visiting after I left my mom's house, though I heard shortly after my mother had a drunken sexual encounter with my uncle jack, which my aunt and uncle worked through, but my mother was black sheeped.

"Ever seen a match burn twice bud?", I flash back to being 5, my father asking me this very serious question. "no sir". I replied knowing even at 5, that when my father wanted your attention, you gave it fully and immediately. He pulled out the box of wooden matches, he maintained his eyes fixed on mine smiling warmly as he pulled a matchstick out of the redbird box and struck it on the side of the box. The match ignited. He said "that's once it is burning now, ready for twice" he asked, and I nodded spell bound by this he blew out the match and very quickly pressed the hot end to the palm of my hand. I screamed the matchstick broke, I was petrified, why did he do that?!? He laughed "and that's twice, now you know a match will burn twice bud". This is how these panic sessions come, a freight train of dread and misery hit me all at once, when it happens I get paralyzed, stuck in one spot, and stuck so far into my own head, so much shame, so much fear, so many questions. For a short time, my parents lived apart and in the same city. I visited my fathers house at least 3 times. With his new woman Kathy. They made me and my sister crawl around on the floors, picking up lint balls off the carpet, every time we visited. I remember the first visit being screamed at for picking my nose and putting it in my pocket. this just never happened, my father imagined it when I was laying on the floor and rubbed my eyes, my pats were sweats, they didn't have pockets. The Kathy lady made candles with us, that was fun, she was a nice lady.

She let me hug her and she hugged me so tightly back. Something weird about my father memories is that I favored him as the better parent often, in reality he was simply nonpartisan, when my dad was around both of us kids were worthless objects unless he felt otherwise for a moment or two. Equally worthless, how bad of a human was I, that I preferred when my sister was suffering equally. Bully or be bullied, with my mom, my sister was the royal princess, and as such she bullied me, hit me often, was overall very mean, and I was the only worthless one everything fell on.

Before my parents split, we lived in Scarborough, Danforth and warden in Toronto. They would kick us out of the apartment when they would fight. Where we lived was one of three high rise buildings. I had friends here, we would roam the hallways when it was rainy or be out in the creek and ravines behind the building during the day. I remember the day my friend Billy Hill, His cousin Donny hill, and myself were in the elevator and this guy was asking us about snakes and if we climber trees, and had we ever climbed the walls. We all were enthusiastically discussing these things while relishing the adult attention I suppose, none of us climbed the walls,

70

and we laughed that we were swimming not going on holidays in our swim shorts. We all got off on one floor and he got us too use our feet and hands to climb up the doorway frames, he would hold a quarter at the top and we climbed to get them. We were young boys in swim shorts, he was of course, a pedophile. We moved to a different doorway and it was the stairwell, he began talking about what buds do after working out and how sometimes our dinks would get hard from being around each other, we laughed and said no, we didn't have boners for each other, he then said, it was ok if we did, but lets find out and he began sticking his hands down all of our pants feeling us up. He began saying "hey do you guys want to see mine, its really big and hard and cool because you guys are being my friend". Billy and I both started getting freaked out and saying "no we have to go, its time to go" but Donny stared as the man exposed himself, and seeing Donny was looking he put Donny's hand on it, "Feels cool, sometimes friends kiss each other's dink when its hard like this to be good friends" he was saying. Billy almost yelled "my dad's going to be checking each for soon we 're leaving and he got Donny's attention with that, and we ran down the hall to the elevators. He never chased us, in hindsight likely escaping to another floor. Billy and I thought we would be in deep trouble if we told anyone we let some stranger touch our dicks, I knew my dad would beat me for that no questions asked, so we all swore a no tell pact. Later that evening unbeknownst to Billy and me, Donny's parents called, and they all met, and police were called, Donny had told his parents. When it was all said and done, the police took the reports, and nothing ever happened, but after they left, I remember my dad saying the strap I was going to get was for lying, talking to strangers, and not putting my clothes on when leaving the pool.

I was sore for days. When I think back, I always wonder why no one but Donny, thanked us for getting him out of their when we did, or said we were smart for getting away. Just that we deserved it for behaving the way we were, talking to strangers. How different times were back then. When I talk with people from my background, we always say things like we were forced to grow up fast, and out the door as a teen. How thankful I am that I had the Chance to protect my children until they truly were responsible adults. How I wish more would have come from my childhood, then the lesson that adults are not to be trusted, so many secrets, so much dysfunction.

I think sometimes I was raised like a stray animal, a feral human, and I think a lot of us are. I think there are a lot of humans mistreating their own due to shear ignorance of self, and alcohol and drug abuse. Its very cute when we as a community can talk of breaking the cycle, but the truth is everyone is just one bad narcissist away, from an incredibly toxic existence.

So, if this was my normal, as a child, am I truly as bad as I am made out to be by those people, for telling the secrets, for refusing to be permanently polluted by their toxins? Attempting to be healthy, to be whole, to be honest to the core, this is supposed to be the way life is experienced, not as an emotionless vessel of deviant dark secrets, being shamed so badly you cant even imagine yourself a victim, but that this is all life has ever had for you.

It is not strength that makes me choose good, it is strength that helps me endure through the bad.

Chapter 12 – Harley Gets a Job

I had to take a deep breath and work some I.T contracts, so I went and worked with Medicentres Canada moving their offices data into the clouds. I had the privilege of doing some weekend gigs, but this past while has been all about visiting with the friends I have made, writing music, trying to get this darn book finished, and growing copious amounts of medical marijuana. The plus was that the entirety of the contract was work from home, so I was able to avoid any professional B.S. lateral violence, and just focus on doing the job.

Having completed the contract, I can say Harley worked that gig. There was no sign of the over aggressive, over ambitious old me. I was simply doing a job to get more money to keep doing what I really want to do.

This has allowed me to see that this will be the final season of my journey, I now will focus on finding one or two communities I can call home, and work within them alone.

I have so enjoyed tripping around Turtle Island, making friends, helping people, crying with people, it has allowed me to just feel o comfortable in my own skin. I no longer wrestle with half breed shame, in the same way we need to stop the cycles of addiction and abuse in our communities, we also need to stop reaffirming the obvious and blaming. No matter what we think Turtle Island will not suddenly have a mass exodus of Europeans returning to their homeland. My father was a horrible human, I don't wear the blame for his actions, so to I no longer wear the blame of my Irish forefathers.

I now feel so connected to the genuine me, and I want to build now. Build relations, family, revenue from doing what I love. Anything else, simply will not do. I had been raised to work to pay bills, never be out of work, now I realize the paying bills is needed of course, but holding out to do what you love is what will make the wait easier.

I now have some lesson plans and strategies to develop to really make this healing hands program work.

Chapter 13 – My True Self Walks

It is autumn 2019, I am doing work up in Western Cree Tribal Council Nations, I facilitate and do healing circles within these nations primarily focusing on Healing through expression (Art Therapy). Even when I started writing this book I realized I was compartmentalizing so many things, within this "Chris Kelly The I.T. Guy, Asshole" and "Harley F. GoodWheeler" and choosing not to address any of the issues as to why I had become who I had become. You see, I am Harley to a good Number of People, but as the months have passed and turned to years, I am seeing I am Human, attach whatever name you need to, but for me, they really matter not. I am a man who has travelled many places, experienced many things, been the savior and the demon, the genius and the idiot, and this is where my growth plateaus to a realization it will take many more years to fully understand, but is easy enough to say.

I am me; everything has led me to the now, this minute, and in this minute, I am me. I can change, grow, shrink, anything I choose, but regardless of what yesterday held, and regardless of what tomorrow brings, today I am me, and I need no validation of being good nor bad, I simply need to feel the way I choose to feel, right now. All good choices come from an unburdened heart.

As this year started, I knew it would be monumental. This was to be the year I decide am I really a healing force? Will I ever get back to full time I.T.? will I find a new Path? So many questions raced through my mind, I did not keep an active log over most of 2019, taking a lot of time to actually heal. A price that gets paid doing the workshops had become clear, I was emotionally in tatters, having re opened so many wounds I never dealt with, in the name of trying to help and heal others. So, some time was spent rebuilding my deck at home, making furniture, sitting by the fire, spending time with family, renovations. I took from roughly June to September off , not booking any work unless very important, it was time to make some conclusions , I felt I couldn't keep going on this path without some resolve, and as I played with my dogs, I thought, and meditated and smudged working maybe one workshop or circle a month.

I need to find my place now, to settle into who I am and again start experiencing new things, as the newer version of myself, in order to do that I had to work through a lifetimes worth of decisions and events, and really understand who I awoke, who I had morphed into needed to be fully explored even by me. During the spring summer, I finished off my training to become a Reiki Master and Instructor. I also sat courses on hypnosis, Mindfulness, Addictions, Psychology, Depression Counselling, Cognitive behavior therapy, Dialectical behavior therapy, Shamanic Life Coaching, European Life Coaching, and Became a 9th degree Grand Master in Right Hand Path Reiki.

I am attaining a level of balance in my life I have never had. Money is a problem this year, a big problem, yet I am happier than I have ever been with myself, and my life.

With the legalization of marijuana here, I have been building out another leg of my business. I offer consulting and teaching for medical marijuana growers, and I am also trying to introduce several products in this area, stone pipes, clips and such, and also organic nutrients designed for growing cannabis.

I was n outlaw grower for years, then decided to get my medical grower papers. Having those I am now trying to find ways to survive in this new reality I have created, healing circles, counselling, consulting, and yes even I.T.

It has finally occurred to me I don't need to abandon everything in my old life, just what I was unhappy with. I don't mind technology, it was the pomp and posture crap I detested, the white way. Still disgusts me, but at the end of the day if I need to fix a pc or move a company to the clouds under my own banner, and my way, I will.

I also sell medicinal herbs and roots, so honestly, I am trying to survive without getting rich or thinking of getting ahead, but with the need for food shelter and gasoline up front and in the open.

I always have weed and can sell small batches to dispensaries if I get really desperate but hoping to not have to travel too far down that road just to subsidize this love for helping, I have developed. I have been on a journey I know won't end, but I have gotten to the part of the path where all I need to do is limit the amount of pain, I expose myself to.

I have thought about my life to date; the metamorphosis I went through/ From small innocent child, to damaged broken youth, to sociopathic criminal, to emotionally abusive narcissist, to beaten and defeated man, to helper, to compassionate soul, to Me in the now. So many faces, so many masks I have worn, addict, dealer, thief, pimp, professional, entrepreneur... I have been these things my entire life, it is a matter of which ones I shine the light on, which things in myself I celebrate instead of condemning.

Many in the world may know right from wrong, I had to learn this in the now, as I go through life. I have recognized the sinister demons, though I rarely hear them anymore, and there are simply choices that are easier and easier to choose the right path, the path for my own health and happiness.

This is all you need to pursue if your guideline is that you will never impact or deter another person's path. You will live love and impact no one in a negative way. Everything gets easier. It is a sad commentary that our country sees two sets of rules to administer, even sadder that in each, there is this rock bottom, never spoken of, class of people so broken and so damaged , that using drugs as an escape seems the most logical choice for anyone living in it. We turn our backs on these people, we brand them with insulting names and titles, I spent the first half of my life as one of them, I spent the next third of my life pretending not to be one of them, and I will spend the last third of my life, being grateful for recognizing that the truth in life and happiness is balancing and acknowledging everyone's unique path. Tolerance. Not tolerance of violence or abuse, tolerance for those who are themselves suffering and hurting others in an effort to make themselves whole. These are the souls we must rain our compassion down onto. Earlier I compared my life to living as a feral human, this to me is exactly what this level of abuse creates. When I try to help or rescue a feral animal, I do not rush at it, I do not pressure it to follow me. I place food down and wait til the animal trusts me enough to eat it, and I keep doing that and over time the animal will come to me when they are ready. This is the same for abused and addicted broken people who have slipped out of society's eye. We need to give them understanding and trust, allowing for them to come and accept it, and then we can begin to help them. The wounds endured can be from abuse, loss of a loved one, neglect, the government interjecting and breaking up a family, those wounds cut the bonds of trust so deeply, that coming back to yourself can be a real challenge. Some of us get lost in addiction and our own ending. Some of us however, rise. Like the phoenix from the flames, we heal, we rise and face the challenge that is this life, and we decide we are going to help anyone who asks in ways we can, to help them learn to trust and love again.

The fear and doubt that permeates our communities our teenagers, and our less fortunate is what needs to be taken on.

Building boundaries so there can be no failure of judgement, then allowing the trust given to be challenged, and accepted. When we teach how to trust and how to remove the fear our scars have left us with this, this is the true way to healing. No mind can be healthy atop a sick body and no body can be healthy under a sick mind. A broken spirit stops all healing. So, the only choice we have to face these times and to heal ourselves is to embrace holism. Mind Body Spirit. To heal in as balanced an approach we can this is how we live and recover.

Healthy food for our bodies, Healthy thoughts for our Minds, Healthy intentions for our Spirit. It is within all of these we slowly rise up and face the human challenge of life again. Let them willingly come from their hiding places within their souls, and warmth and light shall be the free gift all those who aspire for more shall receive.

Seems so easy to write, isn't easy to live, but I have been now for a couple good years. bannock and moose meat stew, healing circles, smudging, planning for a healthy future... all of these combined are what has allowed this transformation to the Harley I am today.

I have a different understanding of my memories then I did when I was struggling. One of my problems seemed to be that I felt like I was nobody, nothing. In times where I had been used or my friendship taken advantage of, I felt like my entire past was a sham, hence if everything ever told me was a lie, then my life was made up of nothing.

I needed to change my thinking, I now look back on times when I have shown love to those who maybe were using me or abusive toward me. I believe my love at the time was true and untainted, and I will not 5rob myself of recognizing that regardless of the actions or intent of others, my love was genuine, from a genuine place, and that leaves me to realize that I was simply taken advantage of while being more vulnerable to someone. Their having a choice to honor that or use it to exploit me, is theirs, as is the burden that goes with it, for me a simple act of loving is the memory I can still stand tall within. It is in those small recognitions I have began to rebuild what was a very broken man. To rethink some of those times and to always give my self my own pat on the back for being pure and honest and real, that is enough, I do not need anyone else to act in this way, it is their choice and their karma should they choose not to act in a humane, responsible way.

This lends itself to far fewer paralyzing days of anxiety and depression. This has offered me at least validation to my on self-existence, and to my choices in life. When you realize everything, you have ever done is your responsibility, quite quickly, you also realize that responsibility is on everyone for themselves only. So if we blame the woman who wore the dress for being raped, logically we then must blame the makers of the clothing, which then logically says we must hold those responsible who make the laws for clothing, who ultimately get elected by us, so we are to blame, everyone but the person who committed the rape? Bad behavior was and will always be bad behavior. We all need to allow he blame to sit where it belongs, accountability matters. And when we do, we have no choice but to move to the next step of healing or closure to the trauma. I once knocked a man out so severely he was placed into a coma, because he asked to borrow a cigarette. I accept my behavior as violent and anti-social. I regret it for those reasons, I live each day knowing that I am trying to pour all kinds of good karma back into the karma bank, to balance this. It takes all kinds of investment of good for me. I spent a long time being the poison. The positive is my belief that what you put in the universe of positive pure intention; you get back 3-fold. This helps me not to feel guilty when I am feeling happy and good in life. The truth of Karma is that it is action based, no words can pretend. But that also means the actions of others do not affect your karma. For example, if I am an asshole you don't get rewarded for it. That's the wrong way to see karma. The good things you do go into the karma bank, and karma reduces the number of negative things that will occur for you. Conversely if you have all kinds of negative karma, an overdraft lets call it; things will not get better for you, everything will also go poorly, until you invest enough into the karma bank to zero out the balance. So, when you invest way more positive than negative your life quality gets better, really easy. It is not the spiteful revengeful bitch of Facebook memes. I like to think to it as; if I am positive for general things it is one for one, but when I help others it is 3 to 1 good karma. This sounds silly I am sure to some, but this balance is for your spirit and to maintain that positive energy needed to then feed the mind and body. It only makes sense when you do it, when you live it, you see it.

Chapter 12 – An Inspiring Woman

Some of this on this journey was spent with a woman. A wonderful Cree angel of a woman, so unknowingly damaged, such a beautiful disaster was she. A relation built on inspiration and living out our dreams, that quickly devolved into two people on different paths, with neither being honest to the changes.

Projection was Amelia's Strongest suit. If I were teaching domestic violence she would be as emotionally abusive as could be. If I were doing anger management, I could count on her provoking me nonstop. Alas several decisions she made were of interest to herself, and damaging to me, I never recovered from this, and spent the last while affording her zero trust for anything, which quickly led to a relationship end.

Amelia was a dreamer, a spiritualist, all the things I was, she was. She could melt me with her smile, and though the relation was truly more toxic than good for far longer than either of us should have tolerated, it was because under all the dysfunction, all the mayhem and chaos, We both believed in each other. There are times in life when we need to leave, or the other person in our life needs to leave to work on themselves. Always allow this, as the resentment will grow til it happens. Its ok to take time away from the responsibilities of being in a partnership if the choice is negative toxic exposure for each other.

They say with great passion comes great fights, I don't speak a lot within this book about this, I will use only this chapter, so as not to cast judgement on Amelia. I do wish her well, but inevitably as my path beckoned me in some different ways, her path led her in different directions. It will always be a shame to me, but it is also something that was allowed to become hurtful, so I don't really dwell on it.

We had initially incorporated companies together, to do workshops and consulting for me, and to do writing and fashion and consulting for Amelia. I owed her a lot as she was the one responsible for that very first meeting discussing domestic abuse workshops, these were her friends then. Soon I realized, and Amelia realized she didn't want to take the kind of risks involved in such a venture, and she went back to work, and this was the beginning of the end. She was very aggressive about advancing the relationship, but when I advanced the relationship, she would buck up and panic and cause duress. Funny really in hindsight, like we sold each other a bill of goods initially, and then changed everything about our lives, but never updated the planning together again. It all wore thin.

One of the things I now see as contributing was that we were both old and tired at the start of this love, we were looking to build our lives to settle own. Heh, soon I think we both realized neither of us were 50 yr old dinosaurs, but we never let one another change, or develop, just hold like granite onto the first promises made, and ride them into oblivion.

Some relations just don't work out. Doesn't mean they were bad. Doesn't mean there needed to be any blame, thing just do not seem to end up working out. For me this was one of those, while I had no regrets, I also knew it had run its course. How strange for me, that this is noteworthy only because she is the first woman I was with when I started this journey, she inspired me with her enthusiasm to see me do it, and after all that has happened, we are still friends. My first ever amicable mature end to a relationship.

You can still search You Tube for Harley F. GoodWheeler and a song titled My Cree Angel, to see just how touched by love I was. Alas, what we both needed was to fall back in love with ourselves, that was our journey together.

It is my hope, she reads this book, and it is also my hope to one day read hers. Kindred spirits for music, and spirituality, but destined to be friends with similar interests.

Chapter 13 – Road trip Files – The Mojave Desert

I took advantage of a sale and decided to go to Nevada for 4 days. I stayed in Las Vegas at the Luxor, but each day toured various parts of the Mojave Desert, hosted and guided by several different tribes. This included a trip to Arizona, the west rim of the Grand Canyon and the Hualapai People. A trip into California and Utah seeing the Joshua tree forest, and to the red rock canyon. I went into the high desert, and also dipped into the low desert. I met and toured with the southern Paiute people and met the Shoshones, some Navajo peoples, some Hopi, and some Washesho people. I went on a dream quest, took some peyote in the desert, which unfortunately didn't hit me til I was back in Vegas, so I did have one nigh ton the strip, all spaced out and tripping balls.

I stood on the edge of the Grand Canyon looking thousands of feet straight down, getting scolded by the rez security guys for not being 5 feet away from the edge.

I got a carving hard stone lesson from an Hualapai elder, after showing him pics of my northern stone arrow heads, we carved stone together and laughed about each other's local stories. For a while I had forgotten how vast this land is, and how we are meek little beings who are gifted our right to be here by a universe that has created everything. This trip was the first out of country trip I had taken since North Carolina; it felt great to finally be on the southern corner of the great plains. soon I will have travelled to each corner, fulfilling a bucket list item for me. I believe my ancestors deserve the respect of visiting all corners of the great plains. I have been fortunate to feel the spirits in the places in the north and the south. When I finally get to finish the 4 directions, I feel I will be somehow completed spiritually, but I have no idea why I think it.

Chapter 14

Before I begin to tell you about the absolute best part of this journey, I have a random thought I need to vent about.

I love the indigenous blood that runs through me. I also love the Irish Heart that pumps it. I have many friends of all origins. Good people are like m and m's they come in all colors with all kinds of differences inside. I speak and teach about residential schools, inter-generational trauma, I am by no means uneducated, nor unaffected, by the tragedies of the past. Hate from history, however, has kept both my cultures hurt and raw. We need to heal now; hate is a thing of the past. I hold no hate. But as a half breed, I catch a fair bit of it.

-As a half breed, I didn't get status money for my education.

-As a half breed, I don't get status health benefits (costs me 200 dollars a month for the most basic coverage)

-As a half breed, I have paid taxes my entire life, thus totaling more than $500,000 dollars of my earnings has gone to pay taxes for programming and roads etc. That benefit everyone.

- I have lost work due to being too light skinned to be taken seriously.

-I have lost work for being too Indigenous in my communications.

All status people claiming white privilege,

and all white people saying indigenous people get a free ride.

Y'all got to stop your racist hate mongering. All of you fucked with each other and I'm the under supported, underfunded, one because of that. All pure bloods of both colors need to shake your damn head and realize how sickening it is to watch privileged people of both origins claiming how rough you have it. we are moving to a one world age where humanity will trump color or creed. I enjoy and take pride in my culture, not recognizing our differences means you do not. Half breeds, the forgotten ones.

The Elders Teach Me

What Does Love Look Like to You?

Ask yourself about this vision

What does Loving your Parents/Elders look like?

What does Loving your Children look like?

What does Loving your Partner/Spouse look like?

Each is a pure, true, honest love; but shown in a way that best offers each unique person, the reflection of what we wish to receive from them. each relation, each unique but pure and true love we have is shown as such.

So how do we show Love for ourselves? What does this look like?

We have such disappointments at times, because we do not feel we receive this love back, but is that just our expectation for someone to show love the way we see it? Much Like my Kokum putting hot food on my plate each day, but never saying, I Love You". She showed me love in her way. One of the things I have learned from very Sage Elders, is that love is always shown, just not always in a way we recognize, and there for, give no recognition. There is pain and hate, all over this planet, so make no mistake there are bad people out there, but when people are caring or listening, when they are feeding you, giving you their time, they are showing love for you in their own way.

I mentioned my workshops, now predominantly are with elders or youth, or full-blown conferences or community engagements. I do not offer the crisis workshops but if asked I will consider it. This is because we need healing in our communities, not more talk about the wounds. The sensitive nature of the disclosures, and the stories, left me in a very poor CPTSD maintenance mode, and I was beginning to break down a bit. So, since the start of 2019 I have focused on healing based sessions, and focused my learning on holistic healing methods and traditional healing, instead. This initially led me down the crisis path, but I have since found my way to mostly healing, through working with Elders and Art Therapy.

This is an area that I have fallen in love with, and while most are either directly Indian residential school survivors, or directly affected by such. The stories I hear and talk through make you burst with tears inside, such cruelty and misery shown to them, and they sometimes share these stories with me for the first time with anyone. To have such grace, and to show me love and respect, this is where I found a lifetime of resiliency, where every terror, every blood curdling, drug induced horror of my past, pales in comparison, and these wonderful humans have simply marched on. Endured. Some comforted by memory blocks, some having never spoke of what they went through, just stoically, they have carried on. I could spend forever being at their beck and call, trying to show and celebrate healthy living to them, it would humbly be the biggest gift the universe could give me.

When I am at home, I play with my dogs, do the housekeeping, Smoke Weed, play guitar, have fires in my backyard. Things I could only procrastinate about for so very long are once again normal.

When I travel up north to work, I am prepared now, but just me, no smoke and mirror boog a boo shit, no lectures or slides, just me interacting with a room full of people I adore, teaching them how to do some crafts and hobbies, and talking about how to make life better. I have special "Clients" ones whom I can see very big changes within the confines of my lens. I try so hard to speak more Cree, the Elders help me, the staff at western Cree tribal council help me. When I am here, I am in my second home. Where I feel my effort to help is seen as help, but not condescending teachings, just people helping people. Community. I live for these communities, one day I will relocate to one, but for now, I need the city and the house as much as I need the community. One day Though, I hope. It is only this journey of self-awakening, that has shown me how to be strong for yourself, I am continuing to try to find all the things I like to do, and find ways to get paid to do them, a concept life would never allow me to do before.

I have been out here, spending my life savings, my retirement, trying to help, and in the end, I came and received help, of a different kind. Help to finally recognize, the joy, the magic in being part of a community.

When I live what I preach, I become the example of what I say. To make that easy, is to simply be the most real me I can be, and that only comes through pure honesty with yourself, and from that your esteem, your attitude, your anger, everything changes so much quicker than you would think.

86

Chapter 15 – Another Random Thought

When I was maybe 17, I lived with 4 underage prostitutes in Toronto, in a hotel on lakeshore boulevard. Charming young criminal I was, I would go and sell drugs and spot license plates for them, beat anyone who messed with them wrong, and such. In exchange they paid for the hotel room, and they all gave me regular payments for a house I was supposed to be saving to buy for us all.

I sold a lot of hash and weed back then, usually making 300 or 400 hundred a day before meals and costs etc. was good money but didn't cover the amount of cocaine I liked to do. Needless to say, every penny I was given I shoved into my arms and kept the bullshit rolling. After a few months two of the girl decided they would "Go Square" and move back home to their parents, I told them they wouldn't get their money ack and they were both ok with that. The two who stayed with me still, Mary and Cheryl, slept in the one bed with me, and most of the daytime fun I remember was sex with all 3 of us. They would tell me they both loved me wanted to live in a house where we all could just get normal jobs and be happy.

One day I got well, fairly itchy down around my groin area, and had a horrible discharge from my penis. Turns out I had gotten Chlamydia and Gonorrhea. I was enraged as the only two women I weas having sex with was Cheryl and Mary. So, someone wasn't using a rubber when they were doing their dates.

Both denied having anything and I insisted we go to a clinic to get them checked. Only Mary and I had had the STD's, Cheryl did not for whatever reason. Mary then admitted she knew she had something, and didn't want to be a prostitute anymore, she was going to go home to Windsor and start a new life. I understood and told her she would not get any money returned. She was not very gracious about that and called from the motel room, two guys she knew to come "Save her" from her violent pimp. and the poor bastards showed up about an hour later. I wasted no time in meeting them outside the motel room door as they pulled up, stabbing he idiot in the passenger seat in the face once then bluntly smashing the handle of the knife against his eyebrow trying to join the hole I put under his eye, to the cut I was creating above it. His friend the driver was smart and started trying to reverse and get the hell out of there, I managed to stab his bud one more time on the top of the leg before the car started pulling out, they even forgot to take Mary with them. I threw about 30 bucks at her and told her go flag a cab, I never saw her again. And as for Cheryl after the clinic, I never saw her again either.

I got thrown out of the motel room, we used one of the girl's id to stay there and they weren't there anymore. I ended up renting another room at a motel next door and the next day was on a greyhound back to Edmonton. and in my addicted had I had a pretty good run for 8 or 9 months getting blasted and not doing much to pay for it.

This is who I was in my youth, if it got me high, I was in. violence? Ha no worries there. Using people? Just part of the lifestyle.

When I got back to Edmonton, I immediately hooked up with some old friends, and started getting high and doing crime. Within a month I was arrested for 32 counts of fraud in Toronto, 21 counts of fraud in Edmonton, an assault, and possession charges. do not collect go, do not collect 200 dollars, and no time to stick any blow up my ass. was a long cold winter.

Chapter 16 – Continuing the awakening

My healing hands workshops have been fairly popular, and I offer 12 different creative activities. I am beginning to sell a reasonable amount of U Carve-It Stone pipes and clips. I am also beginning to see movement selling herbal plants and medicines. I am trying to work the road 12 days a month and do the other stuff in the remaining time. I have opened a division of my company called FR33M4N Farms. I have also completed the development of my organic nutrients. I am by no means getting rich, but I am holding down the bills, and living a life I love. I have learned and put into practice so many Cree based teachings, but most are common to all indigenous people. I am trying to quit smoking, cutting down in recent months from 2 packs to one pack a day. I eat as balanced as I can, but I do count on multivitamins to fill the gap. I meditate daily. I am trying to provide Reiki Healing Sessions in the near future. I have laughed, cried, just all round Lived more, in the last 4 years than in any other period of my life. I have made friends; become known in communities I would've never imagined going and delivering and teaching to. I have had my life in danger, and I have had more joy than I can properly explain. I have felt like a free-wheeling hippie, riding through each day by the seat of my pants, learning as much as I have taught, healing as much as I have healed.

I am a different person, but my soul is the same, I have some freedom from the things that fogged my healing. I choose my own destiny every morning when I wake up. I am healthier than I have been in years, more active than I have been for years. I have made memories that range from tender moments of healing, to passionate late nights with a beautiful woman. I don't regret or even think of things gone by. I trust I made the right choice in the now, and so I don't have to reflect on it. I suffer no worry of the future, deciding what I do as I see fit and doable, I start things early instead of procrastinating and giving my self anxiety.

I have smile lines, instead of worry lines. I cry when I hear sad stories, I laugh when I hear funny things, I have moved so totally out of the fear and shame and worry I was so long plagued with. I had been Judging myself so harshly so often, allowing myself to believe other opinions of me, putting myself up to a measure that never mattered. I found my passion again. I found the reason to live I always needed, and the reason is me. To love myself and treat myself with dignity and respect and compassion. It is my reason to live to reward myself for making the journey to here, the now.

I find the time to do the things I like to do. To make my oils and carve my stone. To play and laugh and lose myself in the pain I used to. I eat right, I sleep 6-8 hrs a night. It isn't that I want to brag, but I do want to impress upon you. Just how important and beneficial it is to your own happiness to grow in the following ways:

Be honest. Stop with excuses or stories twisted to suit who you believe you are. Be honest to yourself of your weaknesses and your strengths, don't hide from yourself, embrace it all as the package that makes you.

Self Doubt, Fear, Anger; these are the leave behinds of trauma or addiction. To get past these we must accept the short comings we have in an honest humble way. It is so important to give yourself the love you deserve, this includes all your pieces. We all have less than perfect parts or behavior, embrace those as the uniqueness that is you.

Healthy living comes from desire. Healing takes work, takes time, takes exploring ourselves to the fullest. One dishonesty in our lives can derail all the work we do on ourselves; I can not state this enough. Honesty with yourself and others is the first change needed if you are to change in a healthy way. Drop all your lies, all your rationalizations of the passed. If you need to, write down what you say everyday, and write down what actions you have taken. Try to really bring what you say down to match your actions. No procrastination, simply words that bring action.

We were raised to be dishonest. All of us. If you question this, here is a few examples:

You don't look fat in those jeans

Adults do not cry

Everything is ok

Three examples of what we get taught as children. We are taught to cater to other egos, at the cost of honesty. Leaving the target of the lie with an unrealistic sense of self potentially, and ourselves with a feeling that is not healthy or a good feeling, because we have lied. So, in order to give them some short-term ego satisfaction, you cost yourself some negativity on your soul. shouldn't you feel good for making someone feel better? Not if it is a lie, no you shouldn't. how about to the question "do I look fat in these jeans?" what if they do look rather uncomplimentary in their jeans, so what. They are seeking re assurance, so a good reply is honesty "you look amazing as the day I met you, I love you". There is an honest answer to what is being looked for in the conversation. For the record ....NO... no person ever asked a question about their own appearance to receive constructive criticism.

This brings up another point about these kinds of encounters, where we can sometimes feel we are being sapped of our compassion. This is because we are so used to telling these little dishonesties, we know them to be wrong, but rarely do we take the few seconds to find a better response than a lie. This where our first tolerances to being dishonest come from. We are taught at a very young age to allow certain dishonesties. We should be being taught how to be tactful and compassionate and honest. I like to pose this as question to people; what is worse? to lie of someone's appearance "you look awesome" or to lie about a crime you have witnessed?

For a lot of us we will answer the second is worse, it's a no brainer. However, both are damaging to equal extents; never underestimate what reducing your own integrity does to your overall health. we carry the burden a lot of shoring up people's self esteem with fake words and lies. We need to be shoring up people's self esteem with honest kindness. They then have their soul fed in a way they needed, and we got to feel good about comforting someone in a very minor way.

So you see, the habits we must change to cleanse ourselves emotionally, mentally and spiritually come from what we have been taught to be as "nice people", when in fact Genuity makes nice people, not harboring lies of various magnitudes. We don't ever need to think back and have new regrets for things we say, part of the changing to be healthier is indeed changing our behaviors to allow less room for bad choices to exist. I will say it one more time, all these choices stem from not being honest with ourselves.

We Learn to understand what healthy food for our bodies is, and we nourish ourselves. We need to nourish our soul, our overall happiness level. We can do this by understanding we should accept no negativity towards us, and we should exude no negativity outward. That is what is meant by impact no one in a negative way. Healthy dialogue for our interactions is what this really translates to; having the mindfulness to not allow conversations to take negative turns.

This is also true for our deep thoughts. We need to keep them cleansed by not allowing self doubt to creep in, when it does change things up, go for a walk or stretch, but change the subject matter of your thoughts to be positive things and force yourself to think in that manner until it is habit.

We are strong even though we sometimes fall.

We are human and mistakes are allowed

Forgiving yourself is not an optional thing, it allows you to stay grounded and humble. It allows you the room to say "I learned something today from my own mistakes. If all we have is negativity and dishonesty and the constant lie of showing, we are perfect in everything we do we become toxic. Because these lies erode the bigger more important healthy thoughts, we need to keep progressing our personal growth.

It feels surreal to me, that it took me so long into my life before I could recognize the damage of ego. How sinister and hidden these lies we tell ourselves are. A moment of feel good, and a forever of carrying one more lie or self denial. A lie is a toxin, you wouldn't build your house on a fresh dump site, so we need to understand that we cant no build our future correctly, ideally for us, if we have toxins hidden in the foundation of us. The hardest part of this is creating that line, that day that you start to say "no more dishonesty with myself or others" ; to stop letting all these trickling little dishonest thoughts or conclusions we have, create uncertainty or insecurity in ourselves and our plans because it makes looking back onto something a regular occurrence. When we become honest with everything, we do not continue to use our ego to protect our lies or carry them forward forever. We do not need to "clean our slate" and suddenly confess every lie we have ever said to ourselves or others, we simply need to pick a day and begin from that point generating nothing dishonest. From that moment on there will be nothing to look back on with regret, as if you conduct yourself with love and respect and compassion all the time, there will be very little doubt in your actions. It also helps with the anxiety stuff as you become confident in saying "I will worry about things as they come up, not before hand'. We lose a lot of our lives worrying about things that simply don't happen, and we need to recognize that time could be spent planning so things won't go wrong for us or doing constructive things to help our Karma bank. There is one statement I use a lot to help with this.

"I can only be responsible for my own happiness, and no one else can make that choice to be happy but me. When we realize this, we change from lying about jeans and looking fat, and start being honest to simply let the person know we love them. Easy stuff to talk about, hard to put into play, but you are strong and determined, and surely can take care of yourself without needing to impact anyone else. The balance to this is that ultimately the person you are lying to, needs truth, not lies.

When we start to be wholly and completely honest, one of the things that occurs is we no longer feel responsible to hold other people's secrets, as they pertain to us. We become completely free of the whole secret, guilt, shame cycle.

My life is becoming a free-spirited ride, and nothing seems to be able to rock my boat, I am such a different person than I was when I started this adventure.

Conclusion - This is where we part my friends

For me, the last few years have been wonderful. My life changed directions and I was able to control that and just see what the universe was saying I should do. I am blessed for this. I am lucky to have decided at some point I could be a better person than I was. I could love others more; I could care about people more; and here I am.

I have spent more time in the last while building flutes, carving stone, building things. Believe when I say the more you work with your hands the more you work through your issues. But balance is the secret.

I am so grateful to be eating at least a meal or two a day that have been home prepared.

I am so grateful for the time afforded to myself to meditate for that even short 5 minutes each day and center myself.

It is so much easier to wake up and worry about today only and getting through it. Plans are easy to make but it's the daily routine that allows you to stick to your planning.

I actually get out and exercise now, walking, doing physical things.

I realize each day that the people who I once felt were hostile, are actually in pain.

I have learned to not judge, but to accept as I need acceptance.

I have looked into the eyes of some of the most abused people I could ever imagine. I have heard stories that would make even the strongest of us wince with horror and disgust. I looked into the eyes of many people you would fear to have in your house, and I helped them.

I will continue to help; it is my calling to work with people in this capacity. And I hope to never lose the passion I found inside myself.

I keep a list daily of mindfulness items, my goals for the day, action items. This stops me from putting things off, it also helps me keep track if I had made any promises to anyone that I fulfill them on time. The more I open up and let people into my life, the more happiness I am finding. The more warmth.

I feel like life is now the way I had always seen it to be on television and movies. That indeed I am not living in a pressure cooker of stress or a vacuum of despair anymore. Light old clothes they were purged, sent to the bin never to be felt by me again.

I sit sweats whenever I can. I believe in traditional beliefs, and I practice my life this way. I do not try to lie about decolonization, because it is just a lie for most. Something to complain just keep mouthing "I need to decolonize". To those people, I say, shut up and do it then. I walked away from everything, I'm still a prisoner of the government so I'm not decolonized, it will take freedom and sovereignty. until we see that as a people, we will continue to only tread water and never actually see our full potential.

I laugh now when I hear racist comments about me. I laugh when I listen to people who used to manipulate me try to now. I laugh when someone says something can't be done, everything imagined can be done, eventually.
Now here is what I stay away from completely for my own healing.
People who gossip
People who steal or lie
People who drink alcohol
People who are not polite to others
People who don't like dogs

I find when I keep these boundaries set as to whether I will even engage a person in my personal life, I find tings go a lot more quietly and stable. With less miscommunications, temper tantrums, just drama dammit, lets call it what it is.

If you are a person who always seems to have a reason to be put out by something, or offended in some way you have an issue in you, I don't need to have that issue in my homelife making things all toxic.

I do not argue. If I am right, I know it, I don't need to prove it to another person. It is just that simple. If you have a differing opinion, I can respect you for that, but if you try to impose your thoughts or opinions onto me, through nonstop chatter, or bullying, or manipulating, I just laugh it off. Can't always get mad that less developed people act in less developed ways, that son them, I don't have time to worry about that in my personal life, that's when I camp and fish and sing and laugh.

One of the things I can say now that I could never admit before is that I was physically and sexually abused. I was victimized as a child. As a man it took me so many decades to just finally grasp that as a little boy, I couldn't defend myself against the bigger threats of adults. They could victimize me then and the bad ones did. I'm not a little child now, I am not a victim now. You can probably still tell me a lie to get my heart strings going and I will fall for it, but I will never ever be the victim I was left to be when I was young.

There is nothing I am really scared of anymore, yet I spend less time blowing my chest up trying to be a tough strong guy. I have learned strength has noting to do with muscles, the Elders I work with each day have shown me this in spades with their strength and eternal spirit to laugh. That is strength.

Being strong is taking care of yourself for yourself

Being strong is caring for others when they can't care for themselves

Being strong is being the person you need or needed in your life at some point, and even though no one was there for you, you choose to stand and be someone else's wall to lean on.

Being strong is being honest, without being hurtful

Most of All Being a strong person is simply living with love respect and compassion, for yourself, and for the rest of the planet.

Caring is what we do when we have no other solution.

I hope you have enjoyed reading about my adventure up until this point. It took me a long time and a lot of gas and bad motel rooms to travel all over and try to find me by helping others. I have heard so much laughter and if not for the respect of confidentiality I would share more here.

I am Harley F. GoodWheeler. I hope t one day get to know those of you who have gotten to know me through this book, do not hesitate to email or contact me.

I will continue on this wonderous path I have carved for myself, selling herbs and medicine, stone carvings, seeds, nutrients, and travelling to nations where my heart resides to deliver workshops, counselling, healing circles, anything I can do to help.

I raise each morning and hope to find someone to share this life with, in time I am sure I will, but for now Like a nomad from times gone by, I will quietly take care of myself, my dogs, and my family, and I will spend my time sharing any knowledge I have with anyone who wants it for their healing benefit.

I will teach arthritis and cancer patients how to grow marijuana organically; I will continue to lobby for more right for medical cannabis users.

In short, I will do what I want, to continue to heal and make my life more meaningful, and I wll find space in everyday, for laughter, for love, and for helping those who need it.

If you liked the read, buy a pipe look for more books from me, schedule a workshop. or imply tell a friend about a good book you read, but don't let them borrow it, I don't pay any bills that way. I speak in jest of course, it has been a pleasure sharing this, from the darkest beds of addiction and failure crawled back into the world and dominated as a cold feelingless i.t. drone. And from their I clawed my way back to being human and feeling things. If a lazy ass weed smoking old biker like me can, you sure as hell bet you can also.

I have delivered now more than 200 workshops, 50 healing circles, 50+ hours of grief or addictions counselling, and have spoken in front of more than 3000 first nation community members in Treaty 8 and treaty 6 territories. I Have travelled 120,000 km in 2.5 years.

I am part of a community, and I am grateful. I know how to heal others, but I needed others to help heal me.

Migwech,
Apihtawikosisan

Acknowledgments

I would like to thank the following people for being in my life in some way while I lived this journey:

Kassandra Kelly – My Daughter for tolerating me through all this travel and looking after my place when I was gone

Nelson Hernandez – For Keeping my sidewalks clean and the fine writers off my back by cutting my lawn

Ann Marie Nipshank – you helped me with a chance to change my life. You may not have realized that was what was happening, but I thank you anyways. I wish for you to find what it is you are searching for and I wish you much success in your writing.

Melody Calahaison - for the work and communication and tirelessly being a friend to me

Edward Wapahoo – because you just make me smile dude

Lisa Vallejo – for taking the time to read some of this book prior to publication for no better reason than to be helpful. Thank You

Erica Jagodinski – for all those gigs

Brenda Goodswimmer – you were an inspiration and you didn't even know it

Lastly, I wish to thank Chief and council in the following nations for their allowing me to come be welcome in their communities:
Whitefish First Nation
Kapawe'no First Nation
Woodland Cree Nation
Driftpile Cree Nation
Bigstone Cree Nation
Pelican Lake First Nation
Sturgeon Lake Cree Nation
Horse Lake Cree Nation

Duncan's First Nation
Sawridge Cree Nation
Sucker Creek First Nation
Loon River First Nation
Lubicon First Nation
(Continued)
Enoch Cree Nation
Montana First Nation
Peerless Trout First Nation
Hualapai Indian Reservation, Arizona.
Northern Paiute Indian Reservation, Nevada

Additionally, I would like to thank the following agencies for their continued support in healing hands therapy:

Western Cree Tribal Council
Keetaskeenow Tribal council
Athabasca Tribal Council
Lesser Slave Indian Regional Council

FR33M4N Enterprise's Consulting Inc.
1-780-760-1552
info@fr33m4n.com